With Christ
in the
School of Prayer

Clarion Classics

With Christ in the School of Prayer

Andrew Murray

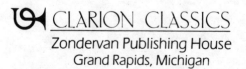
CLARION CLASSICS
Zondervan Publishing House
Grand Rapids, Michigan

Library of Congress Cataloging in Publication Data
Murray, Andrew.
  With Christ in the school of prayer.
  1. Prayer. I. Title.
BV210.2.M83 1983   248.3'2   83-10256
ISBN 0-310-29771-0

Designed by Ann Cherryman

Printed in the United States of America

91   92 / EP / 10   9

Contents

Andrew Murray

Andrew Murray was born in the frontier town of Graaff-Reinet, South Africa, in 1828. He studied in Aberdeen, Scotland and Utrecht, Holland, after which he was ordained a minister in the Dutch Reformed Church. Returning to South Africa, he served in Bloomfontein, Worchester, Cape Town, and Wellington, for a span of more than fifty years. Six times he was the moderator of the Dutch Reformed Church in South Africa. Murray died in 1917, acknowledged as one of the outstanding religious leaders of the nineteenth century in his country.

Murray was a many-sided individual. One of his prime concerns, though little known outside his native South Africa, was in politics. In 1852 he helped organize the Sand River Convention that ultimately led to British recognition of South Africa. Throughout his life he was actively involved in the education and welfare of black South Africans, warning continuously about the dangers of Afrikaner Nationalist political policy that later became the so-called "Christian politics" of Apartheid.

Another interest of Murray's was evangelism. Beginning in 1879 he began a series of seven evangelistic campaigns that were to meet with enormous success. He was impressed by the ministries of Moody and Sankey and tried to organize meetings of his own modeled after them. In the dry and liberalized theological climate of his day, the meetings were like a cool wind blowing over the desert. Thousands of people found their lives changed, some coming to Christ for the first time, others renewing their commitment for service. All of this had a profound effect on Murray who was looking for ways to make the gospel a part of peoples' lives. It was not enough for people to know the correct answers if those correct answers did not penetrate into the essence of their being. Murray was frustrated by shallow acceptance of the faith. These seven campaigns showed him that there was a way to reach the masses with a vital and living Christianity.

Murray was also interested in education. He founded Grey College in 1859 and was its first Rector. This school later became the University of the Orange Free State. He also founded a mission institute in Wellington and was instrumental in starting several other educational institutions.

Perhaps the most important concern of Murray's related to living the Christian life. As were many of his era, he was searching for a way to add depth and vitality to what was fast becoming a lifeless creed. In Murray's case it took the form of a "second blessing" that drew him ever closer to the newly developing pentecostal movement, although the sudden death of a close friend caused him to alter his views rather considerably on the subject of divine healing. He founded an interdenominational prayer union and took an active part in the Student Christian Association of South Africa. His worldwide reputation led to invitations to speak at the famous Keswich Convention in Great Britian and the Northfield Conference in the USA. During his trip to the USA in 1885, he also gave a series of lectures at the Moody Bible Institute in Chicago.

Murray's approach to living the Christian life is that of a practical mysticism. He was influenced by William Law, rather than by speculative German mysticism, and consequently never lost the human touch. He had little time for spiritual indulgence that sought for ever increasing "feelings" of piety. His was a robust faith that took God at His word, requiring that we move out into the world to be light and salt. The secret to being the Christian we ought to be he called "abiding in Christ." By a second act of grace we are to move to another, deeper level of relationship with Christ and remain there by faith. It is an act of total surrender to Christ that allows Christ to become the dominating principle in our lives. When we "abide" we are forever safe, but this is not a static state. For Murray, such words as obedience, absolute surrender, faith, and righteousness (holiness) were very important. All of this implies an active existence.

Murray felt that one of the best ways to reach people was through literature, hence, his constant literary activity. He wrote more than 250 books and numerous articles, being best remembered for *Abide in Christ* (1882), *Absolute Surrender* (1895), and *With Christ in the School of Prayer* (1885).

With Christ in the School of Prayer has become a classic on the subject of prayer. In it Murray attempts to put prayer on a foundation other than that of simply asking and receiving (or not receiving). In it he tries to show that prayer must spring from our inner being as it is united (abiding) with Christ, who is our life. As Christ energizes us, so does He energize our prayer life, giving it a new reality and life. Prayer then becomes the door to the deepest of all spiritual experiences, lifting us up into the very presence of God Himself. When we return to earth, we will never be the same again.

Walter Elwell
Wheaton College
Wheaton, Illinois

Preface

Of all the promises connected with the command, "abide in me," there is none higher, and none that sooner brings the confession, "Not that I have already attained, or am already made perfect," than this: "If ye abide in me, *ask whatsoever ye will, and it shall be done unto you.*" Power with God is the highest attainment of the life of full abiding.

And of all the traits of a life like Christ there is none higher and more glorious than conformity to Him in the work that now engages Him without ceasing in the Father's presence— His all-prevailing intercession. The more we abide in Him, and grow unto His likeness, will His priestly life work in us mightily, and our life become what His is, a life that ever pleads and prevails for men.

"Thou hast made us kings and priests unto God." Both in the king and the priest the power, influence, and blessing is most important. In the king it is the power coming downward; in the priest, the power rising upward, prevailing with God. In our blessed Priest-King, Jesus Christ, the kingly power is founded on the priestly "*He is able* to save to the uttermost, *because* he ever liveth to make intercession." In us, His priests and kings, it is not otherwise: it is in intercession that the church is to find and wield its highest power, that each member of the church is to prove his descent from Israel, who as a prince had power with God and with men, and prevailed.

It is because I am under a deep impression that the place and power of prayer in the Christian life is too little understood, that this book has been written. I feel sure that as long as we look on prayer chiefly as the means of maintaining our own Christian life, we shall not know fully what it is meant to be. But when we learn to regard it as the highest part of the work entrusted to us, the root and strength of all other work, we shall see that there is nothing that we so need to study and practice as the art of praying the right way. If I have at all succeeded in pointing out the progressive teaching of our Lord in regard to prayer, and the distinct reference the wonderful promises of the last night (John 14:16) have to the works we are to do in His Name, to the greater works and to the bearing much fruit, we shall all admit that it is only when the church gives herself up to this holy work of intercession that we can expect the power of Christ to manifest itself in her behalf. It is my prayer that God may use this little book to make clearer to some of His children the wonderful place of power and influence that He is waiting for them to occupy, and for which a weary world is waiting too.

In connection with this there is another truth that has come to me with wonderful clearness as I studied the teaching of Jesus on prayer. It is this: that the Father waits to hear every prayer of faith, to give us whatsoever we will, and whatsoever we ask in Jesus' name. We have become so accustomed to limit the wonderful love and the large promises of our God, that we cannot read the simplest and clearest statements of our Lord without the qualifying clauses by which we guard and expound them. If there is one thing I think the church needs to learn, it is that God means prayer to have an answer, and that it has not entered into the heart of man to conceive what God will do for His child who gives himself to believe that his prayer will be heard. *God hears prayer;* this is a truth universally admitted, but of which very few understand the meaning, or experience the power. If what I have written stirs my reader to go to the Master's words, and take His wondrous promises simply and literally as they stand, my object has been attained.

And then just one thing more. Thousands have found an unspeakable blessing in learning how completely Christ is our life, and how He undertakes to be and to do all in us that we need. I do not know if we have yet learned to apply this truth to our prayer life. Many complain that they do not have the power to pray in faith, to pray the effectual prayer that avails much. The message I would bring them is that the blessed Jesus is waiting, is longing, to teach them this. Christ is our life: in heaven He ever lives to pray; His life in us is an ever-praying life, if we will but trust Him for it. Christ teaches us to pray not only by example, by instruction, by command, by promises, but *by showing us* HIMSELF, *the everliving Intercessor, as our Life.* It is when we believe this, and go and abide in Him for our prayer life too, that our fears of not being able to pray correctly will vanish, and we shall joyfuly and triumphantly trust our Lord to teach us to pray, to be Himself the life and the power of our prayer.

May God open our eyes to see what the holy ministry of intercession is to which, as His royal priesthood, we have been set apart. May He give us a large and strong heart to believe what mighty influence our prayers can exert. And may all fear as to our being able to fulfill our vocation vanish as we see Jesus, living ever to pray, living in us to pray, and standing surety for our prayer life.

ANDREW MURRAY

1 The Only Teacher

And it came to pass, as he was praying in a certain place, that when he ceased, one of his disciples said to him, Lord, teach us to pray.

Luke 11:1

The disciples had been with Christ, and had seen Him pray. They had learned to understand something of the connection between His wondrous life in public, and His secret life of prayer. They had learned to believe in Him as a Master in the art of prayer—none could pray like Him. And so they came to Him with the request, "Lord, teach us to pray." And later they would have told us that there were few things more wonderful or blessed that He taught them than His lessons on prayer.

And now still it comes to pass, as He is praying in a certain place, that disciples who see Him thus engaged feel the need of repeating the same request, "Lord, teach us to pray." As we grow in the Christian life, the thought and the faith of the beloved Master in His never-failing intercession becomes evermore precious, and the hope of being *like Christ* in His intercession gains an attractiveness before unknown. And as we see Him pray, and remember that there is none who can pray like Him, and none who can teach like Him, we feel the petition of the disciples, "Lord, teach us to pray," is just what we need. And as we think how all He is and has, how He Himself is our very own, how He is Himself our life, we feel assured that we have but to ask, and He will be delighted to take us up into closer fellowship with Himself, and teach us to pray even as He prays.

Come, my brothers and sisters! Shall we not go to the blessed

Master and ask Him to enroll our names anew in that school that He always keeps open for those who long to continue their studies in the divine art of prayer and intercession? Yes, let us this very day say to the Master, as they did of old, "Lord, teach us to pray." As we meditate we shall find each word of the petition we bring to be full of meaning.

"Lord, teach us *to pray.*" Yes, *to pray.* This is what we need to be taught. Though in its beginnings prayer is so simple that the feeble child can pray, yet it is at the same time the highest and holiest work to which we can rise. It is fellowship with the Unseen and Most Holy One. The powers of the eternal world have been placed at its disposal. It is the very essence of true religion, the channel of all blessings, the secret of power and life. Not only for ourselves, but for others, for the church, for the world, it is to prayer that God has given the right to take hold of Him and His strength. It is on prayer that the promises wait for their fulfillment, the kingdom for its coming, the glory of God for its full revelation. And for this blessed work, how slothful and unfit we are. Only the Spirit of God can enable us to do it correctly. How speedily we are deceived into a resting in the form, while the power is wanting. Our early training, the teaching of the church, the influence of habit, the stirring of the emotions—how easily these lead to prayer that has no spiritual power, and avails but little. True prayer, which takes hold of God's strength, which avails much, to which the gates of heaven are really opened wide—who would not cry, Oh, for someone to teach me so to pray?

Jesus has opened a school in which He trains His redeemed ones, who especially desire it, to have power in prayer. Shall we not enter it with the petition, Lord! it is just this we need to be taught! O teach us to *pray.*

"Lord, teach *us* to pray." Yes, *us,* Lord. We have read in Your Word with what power Your believing people of old used to pray, and what mighty wonders were done in answer to their prayers. And if this took place under the Old Covenant, in the time of preparation, how much more will You not now, in these days of fulfillment, give Your people this sure sign of Your presence in their midst. We have heard the promises given to Your apostles of the power of prayer in Your name, and have seen how gloriously they experienced their truth: we know for certain, they can become true for us too. We hear continually even in these days what glorious tokens of Your power You still give to those who trust You fully. Lord! these all are men of like passions with ourselves; teach *us* to pray so too. The promises are for us, the powers and gifts of the heavenly world are for us. O teach *us* to pray so that we may receive abundantly. To us too You have entrusted Your work, on our prayer too the coming of Your kingdom depends, in our prayer too You can glorify Your name; "Lord, teach us to pray." Yes, us, Lord; we offer ourselves as learners; we would indeed be taught of You.

"Lord, *teach* us to pray." Yes, we feel the need now of being *taught* to pray. At first nothing appears so simple; later on, nothing that is more difficult; and the confession is forced from us: We do not know how to pray as we ought. It is true we have God's Word, with its clear and sure promises; but sin has so darkened our mind that we do not know always how to apply the Word. In spiritual things we do not always seek the most needful things, or we fail in praying according to the law of the sanctuary. In temporal things we are still less able to avail ourselves of the wonderful liberty our Father has given us to ask what we need. And even when we know what to ask, how much there is still needed to make prayer acceptable. It must be to the glory of God, in full surrender to His will, in full assurance of faith, in the name of Jesus, and with a perseverance that, if need be, refuses to be denied. All this must be learned. It can only be learned in the school of much prayer, for practice makes perfect. Amid the painful consciousness of ignorance and unworthiness, in the struggle between believing and doubting, the heavenly art of effectual prayer is learned. Because, even when we do not remember it, there is One, the Beginner and Finisher of faith and prayer, who watches over our praying, and sees to it that *in all who trust Him for it* their education in the school of prayer shall be carried on to perfection. Let but the deep undertone of all our prayer be the teachableness that comes from a sense of ignorance, and from faith in Him as a perfect teacher, and we may be sure we shall be taught, we shall learn to pray in power. Yes, we may depend upon it, He *teaches* to pray.

"*Lord,* teach us to pray." None can teach like Jesus, none but Jesus; therefore we call on Him to teach us to pray. A pupil needs a teacher who knows his work, who has the gift of teaching, who in patience and love will descend to the pupil's needs. Blessed be God! Jesus is all this and much more. He knows what prayer is. It is Jesus, praying Himself, who teaches how to pray. He learned prayer amid the trials and tears of His earthly life. In heaven it is still His beloved work: His life there is prayer. Nothing delights Him more than to find those whom He can take with Him into the Father's presence, whom He can clothe with power to pray down God's blessing on those around them, whom He can train to be His fellow-workers in the intercession by which the kingdom is to be revealed on earth. He knows how to teach. Now by the urgency of felt need, then by the confidence with which joy inspires. Here by the teaching of the Word, there by the testimony of another believer who knows what it is to have prayer heard. By His Holy Spirit, He has access to our heart, and teaches us to pray by showing us the sin that hinders the prayer, or by giving us the assurance that we please God. He teaches, by giving not only thoughts of what to ask or how to ask, but by breathing within us the very spirit of prayer, by living within us as the Great Intercessor. We may indeed and most joyfully say, "Who teaches like Him?" Jesus never taught His disciples how to preach, only how to pray. He did not speak much of what was needed to preach well, but much of praying well. To know how to speak to God is more than knowing how to speak to man. Not power with men, but power with God is the first thing. Jesus loves to teach us how to pray.

What do you think, my beloved fellow-disciples! would it not be just what we need, to ask the Master for a month to give us a course of special lessons on the art of prayer? As we meditate on the words He spoke on earth, let us yield ourselves to His teaching in the fullest confidence that, with such a teacher, we shall make progress. Let us take time not only to meditate, but to pray, to tarry at the foot of the throne, and be trained to the work of intercession. Let us do so in the assurance that amidst our stammerings and fears He is carrying on His work most beautifully. He will breathe His own life, which is all prayer, into us. As He makes us partakers of His righteousness and His life, He will of His intercession too. As the members of His body, as a holy priesthood, we shall take part in His priestly work of pleading and prevailing with God for men. Yes, let us most joyfully say, ignorant and feeble though we be, "Lord, teach us to pray."

*   *   *   *   *

Blessed Lord! who ever lives to pray, You can teach me too to pray, me to live ever to pray. In this You love to make me share Your glory in heaven, that I should pray without ceasing, and ever stand as a priest in the presence of my God.

Lord Jesus! I ask You this day to enroll my name among those who confess that they know not how to pray as they ought, and especially ask You for a course of teaching in prayer. Lord! teach me to tarry with You in the school, and give You time to train me. May a deep sense of my ignorance, of the wonderful privilege and power of prayer, of the need of the Holy Spirit as the Spirit of prayer, lead me to cast away my thoughts of what I think I know, and make me kneel before You in true teachableness and poverty of spirit.

And fill me, Lord, with the confidence that with such a teacher as You are I shall learn to pray. In the assurance that I have as my teacher, Jesus, who is ever praying to the Father, and by His prayer rules the destinies of His church and the world, I will not be afraid. I need to know of the mysteries of the prayer world, and I know you will unfold them for me. And when I may not know, You will teach me to be strong in faith, giving glory to God.

Blessed Lord! You will not put to shame Your scholar who trusts You, nor, by Your grace, would he shame You either. Amen.

2 *The True Worshipers*

The hour cometh, and now is, when the true worshippers shall worship the Father in spirit and truth: for such doth the Father seek to be his worshippers. God is a Spirit: and they that worship him must worship him in spirit and truth.

John 4:23, 24

These words of Jesus to the woman of Samaria are His first recorded teaching on the subject of prayer. They give us some wonderful first glimpses into the world of prayer. The Father *seeks* worshipers: our worship satisfies His loving heart and is a joy to Him. He seeks *true worshipers*, but doesn't find many such as He would have. True worship is that which is *in spirit and truth.* The Son has come to open the way for this worship in spirit and in truth, and teach it to us. So one of our first lessons in the school of prayer must be to understand what it is to pray in spirit and in truth, and to know how we can attain to it.

To the woman of Samaria our Lord spoke of a threefold worship. There is, first, the ignorant worship of the Samaritans: "Ye worship that which ye know not." The second, the intelligent worship of the Jew, having the true knowledge of God: "We worship that which we know; for salvation is of the Jews." And then the new, the spiritual worship that He Himself has come to introduce: "The hour is coming, and is now, when the true worshippers shall worship the Father in spirit and truth." From the connection it is evident that the words 'in spirit and truth' do not mean, as is often thought, earnestly, from the heart, in sincerity. The Samaritans had the five books of Moses and some knowledge of God; there was doubtless more than one among them who honestly and earnestly sought God in prayer. The Jews had the true full revelation of God in His word, as thus far given; there were among them godly men, who called upon God with their whole heart. And yet not "in spirit and truth," in the full meaning of the words. Jesus says, *"The hour is coming, and now is"*: it is only in and through Him that the worship of God will be in spirit and truth.

Three classes of worshipers can be found among Christians. Some who in their ignorance hardly know what they ask: they pray earnestly, and yet receive but little. There are others who have more correct knowledge, who try to pray with all their mind and heart, and often pray most earnestly, and yet do not attain to the full blessedness of worship in spirit and truth. It is into this third class we must ask our Lord Jesus to take us; we must be taught of Him how to worship in spirit and truth. This alone is spiritual worship; this makes us worshipers such as the Father seeks. In prayer everything will depend on our understanding well and practising the worship in spirit and truth.

"God is *a Spirit* and they that worship him must worship him *in spirit* and truth." The first thought suggested here by the Master is that there must be harmony between God and His worshipers; such as God is, must His worship be. This is according to a principle that prevails throughout the universe: we look for correspondence between an object and the organ to which it reveals or yields itself. The eye has an inner fitness for the light, the ear for sound. The man who would truly worship God, would find and know and possess and enjoy God, must be in harmony with Him, must have a capacity for receiving Him. Because God *is Spirit,* we must worship *in spirit.* As God is, so is His worshiper.

And what does this mean? The woman had asked our Lord whether Samaria or Jerusalem was the true place of worship. He answers that from that day forth worship would no longer be limited to a certain place: "Woman, believe me, *the hour cometh* when neither in this mountain, nor in Jerusalem, shall ye worship the Father." As God is Spirit, not bound by space or time, but in His infinite perfection always and everywhere the same, so His worship would no longer be confined by place or form, but spiritual as God Himself is spiritual—a lesson of deep importance. How much our Christianity suffers from the fact that it is confined to certain times and places. A man who seeks to pray earnestly in the church or in the closet, spends the greater part of the week or the day in a spirit entirely at variance with that in which he prayed. His worship was the work of a fixed place or hour, not of his whole being. God is a spirit: He is the Everlasting and Unchangeable One; what He is, He is always and in truth. Our worship must even so be in spirit and truth: His worship must be the spirit of our life; our life must be worship in spirit as God is Spirit.

"God is a Spirit: and they that worship him must worship him in spirit and truth." The second thought that comes to us is that this worship in the spirit must come from God Himself. God is Spirit: He alone has Spirit to give. It was for this He sent His Son, to fit us for such spiritual worship, by giving us the Holy Spirit. It is of His own work that Jesus speaks when He says twice, "The hour cometh," and then adds, "and is now." He came to baptize with the Holy Spirit; the Spirit could not stream forth until He was glorified (John 1:33, 7:37, 38; 16:7). It was when He had made an end of sin, and had entered into the holiest of all with His blood, and had there on our behalf *received* the Holy Spirit (Acts 2:33), that He could send Him down to us as the Spirit of the Father. It was when Christ had redeemed us, and we in Him had received the position of children, that the Father sent forth the Spirit of His Son into our hearts to cry, 'Abba, Father.' The worship in spirit is the worship of the Father in the Spirit of Christ, the Spirit of Sonship.

This is the reason why Jesus here uses the name of Father. We never find one of the Old Testament saints personally appropriating the name of child or calling God his Father. The worship *of the Father* is possible only to those to whom the Spirit of the Son has been given. The worship *in spirit* is possible only to those to whom the Son has revealed the Father, and who have received the spirit of Sonship. It is only Christ who opens the way and teaches the worship in spirit.

And *in truth.* That does not only mean, *in sincerity.* Nor does it only signify, in accordance with the truth of God's Word. The expression is one of deep and divine meaning. Jesus is "the only-begotten of the Father, *full of* grace and *truth.*" "The law was given by Moses; grace and *truth came* by Jesus Christ." Jesus says, "*I am . . . the truth* and the life." In the Old Testament all was shadow and promise; Jesus brought and gives the reality, *the substance,* of things hoped for. In Him the blessings and powers of the eternal life are our actual possession and experience. Jesus is full of grace and truth; the Holy Spirit is the Spirit of truth; through Him the grace that is in Jesus is ours indeed, and truth is a positive communication out of the divine life. So worship in spirit is worship *in truth*; actual living fellowship with God, a real correspondence and harmony between the Father, who is a Spirit, and the child praying in the spirit.

What Jesus said to the woman of Samaria, she could not at once understand. Pentecost was needed to reveal its full meaning. We are hardly prepared at our first entrance into the school of prayer to grasp such teaching. We shall understand it better later on. Let us only begin and take the lesson as He gives it. We are carnal and cannot bring God the worship He seeks. But Jesus came to give the Spirit: He has given Him to us. Let the disposition in which we set ourselves to pray be what Christ's words have taught us. Let there be the deep confession of our inability to bring God the worship that is pleasing to Him; the childlike teachableness that waits on Him to instruct us; the simple faith that yields itself to the breathing of the Spirit. Above all, let us hold fast the blessed truth—we shall find that the Lord has more to say to us about it—that the knowledge of the fatherhood of God, the revelation of His infinite fatherliness in our hearts, the faith in the infinite love that gives us His Son and His Spirit to make us children, is indeed the secret of prayer in spirit and truth. This is the new and living way Christ opened up for us. To have Christ the Son, and the *Spirit of the Son,* dwelling within us, and revealing the Father, this makes us true, spiritual worshipers.

* * * * *

Blessed Lord! I adore the love with which You did teach a woman, who had refused You a cup of water, what the worship of God must be. I rejoice in the assurance that You will no less now instruct Your disciple, who comes to You with a heart that longs to pray in spirit and in truth. O my Holy Master! do teach me this blessed secret.

Teach me that the worship in spirit and truth is not of man, but only comes from You; that it is not only a thing of times and seasons, but the outflowing of a life in You. Teach me to draw near to God in prayer under the deep impression of my ignorance and my having nothing in myself to offer Him, and at the same time of the provision You, my Savior, make for the Spirit's breathing in my childlike stammerings. I do bless You that in You I am a child, and have a child's liberty of access; that in You I have the spirit of Sonship and of worship of truth. Teach me, above all, blessed Son of the Father, how it is the revelation of the Father that gives confidence in prayer; and let the infinite fatherliness of God's heart be my joy and strength for a life of prayer and of worship. Amen.

3 *Alone With God*

But thou, when thou prayest, enter into thine inner chamber, and having shut thy door, pray to thy Father which is in secret; and thy Father which seeth in secret shall recompense thee.

Matthew 6:6

After Jesus had called His first disciples He gave them their first public teaching in the Sermon on the Mount. He there expounded to them the kingdom of God, its laws and its life. In that kingdom God is not only King, but Father; He not only gives all, but is Himself all. In the knowledge and fellowship of Him alone is its blessedness. Therefore it came as a matter of course that the revelation of prayer and the prayer life was a part of His teaching concerning the new kingdom He came to set up. Moses gave neither command nor regulation with regard to prayer: even the prophets say little directly of the duty of prayer; it is Christ who teaches to pray.

And the first thing the Lord teaches His disciples is that they must have a secret place for prayer; every one must have some solitary spot where he can be alone with his God. Every teacher must have a schoolroom. We have learned to know and accept Jesus as our only teacher in the school of prayer. He has already taught us at Samaria that worship is no longer confined to times and places; that worship, spiritual true worship, is a thing of the spirit and the life; the whole man must in his whole life worship in spirit and truth. And yet He wants each one to choose for himself the fixed spot where He can daily meet him. That inner chamber, that solitary place, is Jesus' schoolroom. That spot may be anywhere; that spot may change from day to day; but that secret place there must be, with the quiet time in which the pupil places himself in the Master's presence, to be by Him prepared to worship the Father. There alone, but there most surely, Jesus comes to us to teach us to pray.

A teacher is always anxious that his schoolroom should be bright and attractive, filled with the light and air of heaven, a place where pupils long to come, and love to stay. In His first words on prayer in the Sermon on the Mount, Jesus seeks to set the inner chamber before us in its most attractive light. If we listen carefully, we soon notice the chief thing He has to tell us of our tarrying there. Three times He uses the name of Father: "Pray to *thy Father*"; "*Thy Father* . . . shall recompense thee"; "*Your Father* knoweth what things ye have need of." First, in closet prayer, I must meet my Father. The light that shines in the closet must be the light of the Father's countenance. The fresh air from heaven with which Jesus would have filled the atmosphere in which I am to breathe and pray, is God's Father-love, His infinite fatherliness. Thus, each thought or petition we breathe out will be simple, hearty, childlike trust in the Father. This is how the Master teaches us to pray: He brings us into the Father's living presence. What we pray there must avail. Let us listen carefully to hear what the Lord has to say to us.

First, *"pray to thy Father which is in secret."* God is a God who hides Himself to the carnal eye. As long as in our worship of God we are chiefly occupied with our own thoughts and exercises, we shall not meet Him who is a Spirit, the unseen One. But to the man who withdraws himself from all that is of the world and man, and prepares to wait upon God alone, the Father will reveal Himself. As he forsakes and gives up and shuts out the world, and the life of the world, and surrenders himself to be led of Christ into the secret of God's presence, the light of the Father's love will rise upon him. The secrecy of the inner chamber and the closed door, the entire separation from all around us, is an image of, and so a help to, that inner spiritual sanctuary, the secret of God's tabernacle, within the veil, where our spirit truly comes into contact with the Invisible One. So we are taught, at the outset of our search after the secret of effectual prayer, to remember that it is in the inner chamber, where we are alone with the Father, that we shall learn to pray correctly. The Father is in secret: in these words Jesus teaches us where He is waiting us, where He is always to be found. Christians often complain that private prayer is not what it should be. They feel weak and sinful, the heart is cold and dark; it is as if they have so little to pray about, and in that little no faith or joy. They are discouraged and kept from prayer by the thought that they cannot come to the Father as they ought or as they wish. Child of God, listen to your Teacher. He tells you that when you go to private prayer your first thought must be: the Father is in secret, the Father waits for me there. Just because your heart is cold and prayerless, get into the presence of the loving Father. As a father pities his children, so the Lord pities you. Do not be thinking of how little you have to bring God, but of how much He wants to give you. Just place yourself before, and look up into, His face; think of His love, His wonderful, tender, pitying love. Just tell Him how sinful and cold and dark all is: it is the Father's loving heart that will give light and warmth to yours. Do what Jesus says: just shut the door, and pray to your Father who is in secret. Is it not wonderful to be able to go alone with God, the infinite God? And then to look up and say: My Father?

"And thy Father, which seeth in secret, will recompense thee." Here Jesus assures us that secret prayer cannot be fruitless: its blessing will show itself in our life. We have but in secret, alone with God, to entrust our life before men to Him; He will reward us openly; He will see to it that the answer to prayer is made manifest in His blessing upon us. Our Lord would thus teach us that as infinite fatherliness and faithfulness is that with which God meets us in secret, so on our part there should be the childlike simplicity of faith, the confidence that our prayer does bring down a blessing. "He that cometh to God must believe that *he is a rewarder* of them that seek him." Not on the strong or the fervent feeling with which I pray does the blessing of the prayer closet depend, but on the love and the power of the Father to whom I there entrust my needs. And therefore the Master has but one de-

sire: Remember your Father is, and sees, and hears in secret; go there and stay there, and go again from there in the confidence that He will recompense. Trust Him for it; depend on Him: prayer to the Father cannot be vain; He will reward you openly.

To further confirm this faith in the Father-love of God, Christ speaks a third word: *"Your Father knoweth what things ye have need of before ye ask him."* At first sight it might appear as if this thought made prayer less needful: God knows far better than we what we need. But as we get a deeper insight into what prayer really is, this truth will help much to strengthen our faith. It will teach us that we do not need, as the heathen, with the multitude and urgency of our words, to compel an unwilling God to listen to us. It will lead to a holy thoughtfulness and silence in prayer as it suggests the question: Does my Father really know that I need this? It will, when once we have been led by the Spirit to the certainty that our request is indeed something that, according to the Word, we need for God's glory, give us wonderful confidence to say, My Father knows I need it and must have it. And if there is any delay in the answer, it will teach us in quiet perseverance to hold on: Father! You know I need it. O the blessed liberty and simplicity of a child that Christ our Teacher would cultivate in us, as we draw near to God: let us look up to the Father until His Spirit works it in us. Let us sometimes in our prayers, when we are in danger of being so occupied with our fervent, urgent petitions, as to forget that the Father knows and hears, let us hold still and just quietly say: My Father sees, my Father hears, my Father knows; it will help our faith to take the answer, and to say: We know that we have the petitions we have asked of Him.

And now, all you who have entered anew the school of Christ to be taught to pray, take these lessons, practice them, and trust Him to perfect you in them. Dwell much in the inner chamber, with the door closed—closed in from men, closed up with God; it is there the Father waits you, it is there Jesus will teach you to pray. To be alone in secret with the Father: this be your highest joy. To be assured that the Father will openly reward the secret prayer, so that it cannot remain unblessed: this be your strength day by day. And to know that the Father knows that you need what you ask, this is your liberty to bring every need, in the assurance that your God will supply it according to His riches in glory in Christ Jesus.

* * * * *

Blessed Savior, with my whole heart I bless You for the appointment of the inner chamber, as the school where You meet each of Your pupils alone, and reveal to him the Father. O my Lord, strengthen my faith so in the Father's tender love and kindness, that as often as I feel sinful or troubled, the first instinctive thought may be to go where I know the Father waits me, and where prayer never can go unblessed. Let the thought that He knows my need before I ask, bring me, in great restfulness of faith, to trust that He will give what His child requires. O let the place of secret prayer become to me the most beloved spot on earth.

And, Lord, hear me as I pray that You would everywhere bless the closets of Your believing people. Let Your wonderful revelation of a Father's tenderness free all young Christians from every thought of secret prayer as a duty or a burden, and lead them to regard it as the highest privilege of their life, a joy and a blessing. Bring back all who are discouraged, because they cannot find anything to bring to You in prayer. O give them to understand that they have only to come with their emptiness to Him who has all to give, and delights to do it. Not, what they have to bring the Father, but what the Father waits to give them, be their one thought.

And bless especially the inner chamber of all Your servants who are working for You, as the place where God's truth and God's grace is revealed to them, where they are daily anointed with fresh oil, where their strength is renewed, and the blessings are received in faith, with which they are to bless their fellow men. Lord, draw us all in the closet nearer to You and the Father. Amen.

4 *The Model Prayer*

After this manner therefore pray ye: Our Father who art in heaven.

Matthew 6:9

Every teacher knows the power of example. He not only tells the child what to do and how to do it, but shows him how it really can be done. In condescension to our weakness, our heavenly Teacher has given us the very words we are to take with us as we draw near to our Father. We have in them a form of prayer in which there breathes the freshness and fullness of the eternal life—so simple that the child can lisp it, so divinely rich that it comprehends all that God can give. It is a form of prayer that becomes the model and inspiration for all other prayer, and yet always draws us back to itself as the deepest utterance of our souls before our God.

"Our Father who art in heaven!" To appreciate this word of adoration as we ought, I must remember that none of the saints in Scripture had ever ventured to address God as their Father. The invocation places us at once in the center of the wonderful revelation the Son came to make of His Father as our Father too. It comprehends the mystery of redemption—Christ delivering us from the curse that we might become the children of God. The mystery of regeneration—the Spirit in the new birth giving us the new life. And the mystery of faith—before the redemption is accomplished or understood, the word is given on the lips of the disciples to prepare them for the blessed experience still to come. The words are the key to the whole prayer, to all prayer. It takes time, it takes a whole lifetime to study them; it will take eternity to understand

16

them fully. The knowledge of God's Father-love is the first and simplest, but also the last and highest lesson in the school of prayer. It is in the personal relation to the living God, and the personal conscious fellowship of love with Himself, that prayer begins. It is in the knowledge of God's fatherliness, revealed by the Holy Spirit, that the power of prayer will be found to root and grow. In the infinite tenderness and pity and patience of the infinite Father, in His loving readiness to hear and to help, the life of prayer has its joy. O let us take time, until the Spirit has made these words to us spirit and truth, filling heart and life: "Our Father who art in heaven." Then we are indeed within the veil, in the secret place of power where prayer always prevails.

"Hallowed be thy name." There is something here that strikes us at once. While we ordinarily first bring our own needs to God in prayer, and then think of what belongs to God and His interests, the Master reverses the order. First, *thy* name, *thy* kingdom, *thy* will; then, give *us*, forgive *us*, lead *us*, deliver *us*. The lesson is of more importance than we think. In true worship the Father must be first, must be all. The sooner I learn to forget myself in the desire that He may be glorified, the richer will the blessing be that prayer will bring to myself. No one ever loses by what he sacrifices for the Father.

This must influence all our prayer. There are two sorts of prayer: personal and intercessory. The latter ordinarily occupies the lesser part of our time and energy. This may not be. Christ has opened the school of prayer especially to train intercessors for the great work of bringing down, by their faith and prayer, the blessings of His work and love on the world around. There can be no deep growth in prayer unless this be made our aim. The little child may ask of the father only what it needs for itself; and yet it soon learns to ask for some for his sister too. But the grown-up son, who lives only for the father's interest and takes charge of the father's business, asks for more, and gets all that is asked. And Jesus would train us to the blessed life of consecration and service, in which our interests are all subordinate to the name, and the kingdom, and the will of the Father. O let us live for this, and, on each act of adoration, Our Father, let there follow in the same breath, *thy* Name, *thy* Kingdom, *thy* Will—for this we look up and long.

What name are we to hallow? This new name of Father. The word *holy* is the central word of the Old Testament; the *name* Father of the new. In this name of love all the holiness and glory of God are now to be revealed. And how is the name to be hallowed? By God Himself: "*I will hallow My great name which you have profaned.*" *Our prayer must be that in ourselves, in all God's children, in presence of the world, God Himself would reveal the holiness, the divine power, the hidden glory of the name of Father. The Spirit of the Father is the Holy* Spirit: it is only when we yield ourselves to be led *of Him,* that the name will be *hallowed* in our prayer and our lives. Let us learn the prayer: "Our Father, hallowed be thy name."

"*Thy kingdom come.*" The Father is a King and has a kingdom. The son and heir of a king has no higher ambition than the glory of his father's kingdom. In time of war or danger this becomes his passion; he can think of nothing else. The children of the Father are here in the enemy's territory, where the kingdom, which is in heaven, is not yet fully manifested. What is more natural than that when they learn to hallow the Father-name, they should long for and cry with deep enthusiasm: "Thy kingdom come." The coming of the kingdom is the one great event on which the revelation of the Father's glory, the blessedness of His children, the salvation of the world depends. On our prayers too the coming of the kingdom waits. Shall we not join in the deep longing cry of the redeemed: "Thy kingdom come"? Let us learn it in the school of Jesus.

"*Thy will be done, as in heaven, so on earth.*" This petition is too frequently applied alone to the *suffering* of the will of God. In heaven God's will is *done,* and the Master teaches the child to ask that the will may be done on earth just as in heaven: in the spirit of adoring submission and ready obedience. Because the will of God is the glory of heaven, the doing of it is the blessedness of heaven. As the will is done, the kingdom of heaven comes into the heart. And wherever faith has accepted the Father's love, obedience accepts the Father's will. The surrender to, and the prayer for a life of heaven-like obedience, is the spirit of childlike prayer.

"Give us this day our daily bread." When first the child had yielded himself to the Father in the care for His name, His kingdom, and His will, he has full liberty to ask for his daily bread. A master provides for the food of his servant, a general for his soldiers, a father for his child. And will not the Father in heaven care for the child who has in prayer given himself up to His interests? We may indeed in full confidence say: Father, I live for Your honor and Your work; I know You care for me. Consecration to God and His will gives wonderful liberty in prayer for temporal things: the whole earthly life is given to the Father's loving care.

"And forgive us our debts, as we also have forgiven our debtors." As bread is the first need of the body, so forgiveness is of the soul. And the provision for the one is as sure as for the other. We are children, but sinners too; our right of access to the Father's presence we owe to the precious blood and the forgiveness it has won for us. Let us beware of the prayer for forgiveness becoming a formality: only what is really confessed is really forgiven. Let us in faith accept the forgiveness as promised: as a spiritual reality, an actual transaction between God and us, it is the entrance into all the Father's love and all the privileges of children. Such forgiveness, as a living experience, is impossible without a forgiving spirit to others: as *forgiven* expresses the heavenward, so *forgiving* the earthward, relation of God's child. In each prayer to the Father I must be able to say that I know of no one whom I do not heartily love.

"And bring us not into temptation, but deliver us from the evil one." Our daily bread, the pardon of our sins, and then our being kept from all sin and the power of the evil one, in these three petitions all our personal need is comprehended. The prayer for bread and pardon must be accompanied by the surrender to live in all things in holy obedience to the Father's will, and the believing prayer in everything to be kept by the power of the indwelling Spirit from the power of the evil one.

Children of God, it is this way Jesus would have us to pray

to the Father in heaven. O let His name, and kingdom, and will, have the first place in our love; His providing, and pardoning, and keeping love will be our sure portion. So the prayer will lead us up to the true child-life: the Father all to the child, the Father all for the child. We shall understand how Father and child, the *thine* and the *our,* are all one, and how the heart that begins its prayer with the God-devoted THINE, will have the power in faith to speak out the OUR too. Such prayer will indeed be the fellowship and interchange of love, always bringing us back in trust and worship to Him who is not only the Beginning but also the End: "For thine is the kingdom, and the power, and the glory, for ever, Amen." Son of the Father, teach us to pray, "Our Father."

* * * * *

O You who are the only-begotten Son, teach us, we beseech You, to pray, "Our Father." We thank You, Lord, for these living blessed words that you have given us. We thank You for the millions who in them have learned to know and worship the Father, and for what they have been to us. Lord, it is as if we needed days and weeks in Your school with each separate petition; so deep and full they are. But we look to You to lead us deeper into their meaning: do it, we pray You, for Your name's sake; Your name is Son of the Father.

Lord! You once said: "No man knoweth the Father save the Son, and he to whom the Son willeth to reveal him." And again: "I made known unto them thy name, and will make it known, that the love wherewith thou hast loved me may be in them." Lord Jesus, reveal to us the Father. Let His name, His infinite Father-love, the love with which He loved You, according to Your prayer, be in us. Then shall we say aright, "Our Father!" Then shall we apprehend Your teaching, and the first spontaneous breathing of our heart will be: "Our Father, Your name, Your kingdom, Your will." And we shall bring our needs and our sins and our temptations to Him in the confidence that the love of such a Father cares for all.

Blessed Lord, we are Your scholars, we trust you; do teach us to pray, "Our Father." Amen.

5 The Certainty of the Answer to Prayer

Ask, and it shall *be given you; seek, and ye* shall *find; knock, and it* shall *be opened unto you: for every one that asketh* receiveth, *and he that seeketh* findeth; *and to him that knocketh it* shall be opened.

Matthew 7:7, 8

Ye ask, and receive not, *because ye ask amiss.*

James 4:3

Our Lord returns here in the Sermon on the Mount a second time to speak of prayer. The first time He had spoken of the Father who is to be found in secret, and rewards openly, and had given us the pattern prayer (Matt. 6:5-15). Here He wants to teach us what in all Scripture is considered the chief blessing in prayer: the assurance that prayer will be heard and answered. Observe how He uses words that mean almost the same thing, and each time repeats the promise so distinctly: "Ye *shall* receive, ye *shall* find, it *shall* be opened unto you"; and then gives as ground for such assurance the law of the kingdom: "Everyone that asketh, *receiveth*; he that seeketh *findeth*; and to him that knocketh *it shall be opened.*" We cannot but feel how in this sixfold repetition He wants to impress deep on our minds this one truth, that we may and must most confidently expect an answer to our prayer. Next to the revelation of the Father's love, there is, in the whole course of the school of prayer, not a more important lesson than this: every one who asks, receives.

In the three words the Lord uses, *ask, seek, knock,* a difference in meaning has been sought. If such was indeed His purpose, then Ask refers to the gifts we pray for. But I may ask and receive the gift without the Giver. Seek is the word Scripture uses of God Himself; Christ assures me that I can find Himself. But it is not enough to find God in time of need, without coming to abiding fellowship: Knock speaks of admission to dwell with Him and in Him. Asking and receiving the gift would thus lead to seeking and finding the Giver, and this again to the knocking and opening of the door of the Father's home and love. One thing is sure: the Lord does want us to count on the fact that asking, seeking, and knocking, cannot be in vain: receiving an answer, finding God, the opened heart and home of God, are the certain fruit of prayer.

That the Lord should have thought it needful in so many forms to repeat the truth, is a lesson of great importance. It proves that He knows our heart, how doubt and distrust toward God are natural to us, and how easily we are inclined to rest in prayer as a religious work without an answer. He also knows how even when we believe that God is the hearer of prayer, believing prayer that lays hold of the promise is something spiritual, too high and difficult for the half-hearted disciple. He therefore at the outset of His instruction to those who would learn to pray, seeks to impress this truth deep into their hearts: prayer does avail much; ask and ye *shall* receive; *every one* that asks, receives. This is the fixed eternal law of the kingdom: if you ask and do not receive, it must be because there is something amiss or wanting in the prayer. Hold on; let the Word and Spirit teach you to pray in the right way, but do not let go the confidence He seeks to waken: Every one who asks, receives.

"Ask, and it shall be given you." Christ has no mightier stimulus to preserving prayer in His school than this. As a child has to prove a sum to be correct, so the proof that we have prayed as we ought is *the answer.* If we ask and do not receive, it is because we have not learned to pray correctly. Let every learner in the school of Christ therefore take the Master's word in all simplicity: every one who asks, receives. He had good reasons for speaking so unconditionally. Let us beware of weakening the Word with our human wisdom. When He tells us heavenly things, let us believe Him: His Word will explain itself to him who believes it fully. If questions and

difficulties arise, let us not seek to have them settled before we accept the Word. No, let us entrust them all to Him; He will solve them; our work is first and fully to accept and hold fast His promise. In our inner chamber, in the inner chamber of our heart too, let the word be inscribed in letters of light: every one who asks, receives.

According to this teaching of the Master, prayer consists of two parts, has two sides, human and divine. The human is the asking, the divine is the giving. Or, to look at both from the human side, there is the asking and the receiving—the two halves that make up a whole. It is as if He would tell us that we are not to rest without an answer, because it is the will of God, the rule in the Father's family that every childlike believing petition is granted. If no answer comes, we are not to sit down in the sloth that calls itself resignation, and suppose that it is not God's will to give an answer. No; there must be something in the prayer that is not as God would have it, childlike and believing; we must seek for grace to pray so that the answer may come. It is far easier for the flesh to submit without the answer than to yield itself to be searched and purified by the Spirit, until it has learned to pray the prayer of faith.

It is one of the terrible marks of the diseased state of Christian life these days that there are so many who rest content without the distinct experience of answer to prayer. They pray daily, they ask many things, and trust that some of them will be heard, but know little of direct definite answer to prayer as the rule of daily life. But the will of the Father is to seek daily intercourse with His children in listening to and granting their petitions. He wills that I should come to Him day by day with distinct requests; He wills day by day to do for me what I ask. It was in His answer to prayer that the saints of old learned to know God as the Living One, and were stirred to praise and love (Pss. 34; 66:19; 116:1). Our Teacher waits to imprint this upon our minds: prayer and its answer, the child asking and the father giving, belong to each other.

There may be cases in which the answer is a refusal because the request is not according to God's word, as when Moses asked to enter Canaan. But still, there was an answer: God did not leave His servant in uncertainty as to His will. The gods of the heathen are dumb and cannot speak. Our Father lets His child know when He cannot give him what he asks, and he withdraws his petition, even as the Son did in Gethsemane. Both Moses the servant and Christ the Son knew that what they asked was not according to what the Lord had spoken: their prayer was the humble supplication even if it was not possible for the decision to be changed. God will teach those who are teachable and give Him time, by His Word and Spirit, to see whether their request is according to His will or not. Let us withdraw the request, if it is not according to God's mind, or persevere until the answer comes. Prayer is appointed to obtain the answer. It is in prayer and its answer that the interchange of love between the Father and His child takes place.

How deep the estrangement of our heart from God must be if we find it so difficult to grasp such promises. Even while we accept the words and believe their truth, the faith of the heart, that fully has them and rejoices in them, comes so slowly. It is because our spiritual life is still so weak, and the capacity for taking God's thoughts is so feeble. But let us look to Jesus to teach us as none but He can teach. If we take His words in simplicity, and trust Him by His Spirit to make them within us life and power, they will so enter into our inner being that the spiritual divine reality of the truth they contain will indeed take possession of us, and we shall not rest content until every petition we offer is borne heavenward on Jesus' own words: "Ask, and it shall be given you."

Beloved fellow-disciples in the school of Jesus, let us set ourselves to learn this lesson well. Let us take these words just as they were spoken. Let us not suffer human reason to weaken their force. Let us take them as Jesus gives them, and believe them. He will teach us in due time how to understand them fully: let us begin by implicitly believing them. Let us take time, as often as we pray, to listen to His voice: every one who asks, receives. Let us not make the feeble experiences of our unbelief the measure of what our faith may expect. Let us seek, not only just in our seasons of prayer, but at all times, to hold fast the joyful assurance that man's prayer on earth and God's answer in heaven are meant for each other. Let us trust Jesus to teach us so to pray, that the answer can come. He will do it, if we hold fast to the word He gives today: "Ask, and ye shall receive."

* * * * *

O Lord Jesus! teach me to understand and believe what You have now promised me. It is not hid from You, O my Lord, with what reasonings my heart seeks to satisfy itself, when no answer comes. There is the thought that my prayer is not in harmony with the Father's secret counsel; that there is perhaps something better You would give me; or that prayer as fellowship with God is blessing enough without an answer. And yet, my blessed Lord, I find in Your teaching on prayer that You did not speak of these things, but said so plainly, that prayer may and must expect an answer. You assure us that this is the fellowship of the child with the Father: the child asks and the Father gives.

Blessed Lord! Your words are faithful and true. It must be, because I pray amiss, that my experience of answered prayer is not clearer. It must be, because I live too little in the Spirit, that my prayer is too little in the Spirit, and that the power for the prayer of faith is wanting.

Lord! teach me to pray. Lord Jesus! I trust You for it; teach me to pray in faith. Lord! teach me this lesson of today: Every one who asks, receives. Amen.

6 The Infinite Fatherliness of God

Or what man is there of you, who, if his son shall ask him for a loaf, will give him a stone; or if he shall ask for a fish, will give him a serpent? If ye then, being evil, know how to give good gifts unto your children, how much more shall your Father who is in heaven give good things to them that ask him?

Matthew 7:9-11

In these words our Lord proceeds further to confirm what He had said of the certainty of an answer to prayer. To remove all doubt, and show us on what sure ground His promise rests, He appeals to what every one has seen and experienced here on earth. We are all children, and know what we expected of our fathers. We are fathers, or continually see them; and everywhere we look upon it as the most natural thing there can be that a father hear his child. And the Lord asks us to look up from earthly parents, of whom the best are but evil, and to calculate how much more the heavenly Father will give good gifts to those who ask Him. Jesus would have us to see that as much greater as God is than sinful man, *so much greater* our assurance ought to be that He will more surely than any earthly father grant our childlike petitions. As much greater as God is than man, *so much surer* is it that prayer will be heard with the Father in heaven than with a father on earth.

As simple and intelligible as this parable is, so deep and spiritual is the teaching it contains. The Lord would remind us that the prayer of a child owes its influence entirely to the relation in which he stands to the parent. The prayer can exert that influence only when the child is really living in that relationship, in the home, in the love, in the service of the Father. The power of the promise, "Ask, and it shall be given you," lies in the loving relationship between us as children and the Father in heaven; when we live and walk in that relationship, the prayer of faith and its answer will be the natural result. And so the lesson we have today in the school of prayer is this: Live as a child of God, then you will be able to pray as a child, and as a child you will most assuredly be heard.

And what is the true child life? The answer can be found in any home. The child that by preference forsakes the father's house, that finds no pleasure in the presence and love and obedience of the father, and still thinks to ask what he will, will surely be disappointed. On the contrary, he to whom the intercourse and will and honor and love of the father are the joy of his life, will find that it is the father's joy to grant his requests. Scripture says, "As many as are *led* by the Spirit of God, they are the children of God": the childlike privilege of asking all is inseparable from the childlike life under the leading of the Spirit. He who gives himself to be led by the Spirit in his life, will be led by Him in his prayers too. And he will find that Fatherlike giving is the divine response to childlike living.

To see what this childlike living is, in which childlike asking and believing have their ground, we have only to notice what our Lord teaches in the Sermon on the Mount of the Father and His children. In it the prayer promises are imbedded in life precepts; the two are inseparable. They form one whole; and He alone can count on the fulfillment of the promise, who accepts too all that the Lord has connected with it. It is as if in speaking the word, "Ask, and ye shall receive," He says: I give these promises to those whom in the beatitudes I have pictured in their childlike poverty and purity, and of whom I have said, "They shall be called the children of God" (Matt. 5:3-9): to children, who "let your light shine before men, so that they may glorify your Father in heaven": to those who walk in love, "that ye may be children of your Father which is in heaven," and who seek to be perfect "even as your Father

in heaven is perfect" (6:45): to those whose fasting and praying and almsgiving (6:1-18) is not before men, but "before
your Father which seeth in secret," who forgive "even as your
Father forgiveth you" (6:15); who trust the heavenly Father in
all earthly need, seeking first the kingdom of God and His
righteousness (6:22-26); who not only say, Lord, Lord, but do
the will of my Father which is in heaven (7:21). Such are the
children of the Father, and such is the life in the Father's love
and service; in such a child-life answered prayers are certain
and abundant.

But will not such teaching discourage the feeble one? If we
are first to answer to this portrait of a child, must not many
give up all hope of answers to prayer? The difficulty is removed if we think again of the blessed name of father and
child. A child is weak; there is a great difference among children in age and gift. The Lord does not demand of us a perfect
fulfillment of the law; no, but only the childlike and wholehearted surrender to live as a child with Him in obedience
and truth. Nothing more. But also, nothing less. The Father
must have the whole heart. When this is given, and He sees
the child with honest purpose and steady will seeking in
everything to be and live as a child, then our prayer will count
with Him as the prayer of a child. Let any one simply and
honestly begin to study the Sermon on the Mount and take
it as his guide in life, and he will find, notwithstanding weakness and failure, an evergrowing liberty to claim the fulfillment of its promises in regard to prayer. In the names of
father and child he has the pledge that his petitions will be
granted.

This is the one chief thought on which Jesus dwells here,
and which He would have all His scholars take in. He would
have us see that the secret of effectual prayer is to have the
heart filled with the Father-love of God. It is not enough for
us to know that God is a Father: He would have us take time
to come under the full impression of what that implies. We
must take the best earthly father we know; think of the tenderness and love with which he regards the request of his
child, the love and joy with which he grants every reasonable
desire; then, as we think in adoring worship of the infinite

love and fatherliness of God, consider with *how much more* tenderness and joy *He* sees us come to Him, and gives us what we ask aright. And then, when we see how much this divine arithmetic is beyond our comprehension, and feel how impossible it is for us to apprehend God's readiness to hear us, then He would have us come and open our heart for the Holy Spirit to shed abroad God's Father-love there. Let us do this not only when we want to pray, but let us also yield heart and life to dwell in that love. The child who wants only to know the love of the father when he has something to ask, will be disappointed. But he who lets God be Father always and in everything, who would live his whole life in the Father's presence and love, who allows God in all the greatness of His love to be a Father to him, he will experience most gloriously that a life in God's infinite fatherliness and continual answers to prayer are inseparable.

Beloved fellow disciple, we begin to see the reason why we know so little of daily answers to prayer, and what the chief lesson is that the Lord has for us in His school. It is all in the name of Father. We thought of new and deeper insight into some of the mysteries of the prayer world as what we should get in Christ's school; He tells us the first is the highest lesson; we must learn to say well, "Abba, Father!" "Our Father who art in heaven." He who can say this has the key to all prayer. In all the compassion with which a father listens to his weak or sickly child, in all the joy with which he hears his stammering child, in all the gentle patience with which he bears with a thoughtless child, we must, as in so many mirrors, study the heart of our Father, until every prayer be borne upward on the faith of this divine word: "*How much more* shall your Father who is in heaven give good things to them that ask him."

*   *   *   *   *

Blessed Lord! You know that this, though it be one of the first and simplest and most glorious lessons in Your school, is to our hearts one of the hardest to learn: we know so little of the love of the Father. Lord, teach us so to live with the Father that His love may be to us nearer, clearer, dearer, than the love of any earthly father. And let the assurance of His hearing our prayer be as much greater than the confidence in an earthly parent, as the heavens are higher than earth, as God is infinitely greater than man. Lord, show us that it is only our unchildlike distance from the Father that hinders the answer to prayer, and lead us on to the true life of God's children. Lord Jesus, it is fatherlike love that wakens childlike trust. Reveal to us the Father, and His tender, pitying love, that we may become childlike, and experience how in this lies the power of prayer.

Blessed Son of God, the Father loves You and has given You all things. And You love the Father, and have done all things He commanded You, and therefore have the power to ask all things. Lord, give us Your own Spirit, the Spirit of the Son. Make us childlike, as You were on earth. And let every prayer be breathed in the faith that as the heaven is higher than the earth, so God's Father-love, and His readiness to give us what we ask, suppasses all we can think or conceive. Amen.

7 The All-Comprehensive Gift

If ye then, being evil, know how to give good gifts unto your children, how much more shall Your heavenly Father give the Holy Spirit to them that ask him?

Luke 11:13

In the Sermon on the Mount, the Lord had already given utterance to His wonderful "How much more?" Here in Luke, where He repeats the question, there is a difference. Instead of speaking, as then, of giving *good gifts*, He says, "How much more shall your heavenly Father give *the Holy Spirit*?" He therefore teaches us that the chief and the best of these gifts is the Holy Spirit, or rather, that in this gift all others are comprised. The Holy Spirit is the first of the Father's gifts, and the one He delights most to bestow. The Holy Spirit is therefore the gift we ought first and chiefly to seek.

The unspeakable worth of this gift we can easily understand. Jesus spoke of the Spirit as "*the* promise of the Father"; the one promise in which God's fatherhood revealed itself. The best gift a good and wise father can bestow on a child on earth is his own spirit. This is the great object of a father in education—to reproduce in his child his own disposition and character. If the child is to know and understand his father; if, as he grows up, he is to enter into all his will and plans; if he is to have his highest joy in the father, and the father in him—he must be of one mind and spirit with him. So it is impossible to conceive of God bestowing any higher gift on His child than this, His own Spirit. God is what He is through His Spirit; the Spirit is the very life of God.

Just think what it means—God giving His own Spirit to His child on earth.

Was this not the glory of Jesus as a Son on earth, that the Spirit of the Father was in Him? At His baptism in Jordan two things were united—the voice, proclaiming Him the beloved Son, and the Spirit, descending on Him. So the apostle says of us, "Because ye are sons, God sent forth the Spirit of his Son into our hearts, crying, Abba, Father." A king seeks in the complete education of his son to call forth in him a kingly spirit. Our Father in heaven desires to educate us as His children for the holy, heavenly life in which He dwells, and for this gives us, from the depths of His heart, His own Spirit. This was the aim of Jesus when, after having made atonement with His own blood, He entered for us into God's presence, that He might attain for us, and send down the Holy Spirit to dwell in us. As the Spirit of the Father and of the Son, the whole life and love of the Father and the Son are in Him; and, coming down into us, He lifts us up into their fellowship. As Spirit of the Father, He sheds abroad the Father's love, with which He loved the Son, in our hearts, and teaches us to live in it. As Spirit of the Son, He breathes in us the childlike liberty, and devotion, and obedience in which the Son lived on earth. The Father can bestow no higher or more wonderful gift than this: His own Holy Spirit, the Spirit of sonship.

This truth naturally suggests the thought that this first and chief gift of God must be the first and chief object of all prayer. For every need of the spiritual life this is the one thing needful: the Holy Spirit. All the fullness is in Jesus; the fullness of grace and truth, out of which we receive grace for grace. The Holy Spirit is the appointed conveyance, whose special work it is to make Jesus and all there is in Him for us ours in personal appropriation, in blessed experience. He is the Spirit of life in Christ Jesus. As wonderful as the life is, more wonderful is the provision by which such an agent is provided to communicate it to us. If we but yield ourselves entirely to the disposal of the Spirit, and let Him have His way with us, He will manifest the life of Christ within us. He will do this with a divine power, maintaining the life of Christ in us in uninterrupted continuity. Surely, if there is one prayer that should draw us to the Father's heart and keep us there, it is that the Holy Spirit, whom we as children have received, may stream into us and out from us in greater fullness. In the variety of the gifts which the Spirit has to dispense, He meets the believer's every need. Just think of the names He bears: the Spirit of grace, to reveal and impart all of grace there is in Jesus; the Spirit of faith, teaching us to begin and go on and increase in ever believing; the Spirit of adoption and assurance, who witnesses that we are God's children, and inspires the confiding and confident Abba, Father!; the Spirit of truth, to lead into all truth, to make each word of God ours in deed and in truth; the Spirit of prayer, through whom we speak with the Father, prayer that must be heard; the Spirit of judgment and burning, to search the heart and convince of sin; the Spirit of holiness, manifesting and communicating the Father's holy presence within us; the Spirit of power, through whom we are strong to testify boldly and work effectually in the Father's service; the Spirit of glory, the pledge of our inheritance, the preparation and the foretaste of the glory to come. Surely the child of God needs but one thing to be able really to live as a child: it is to be filled with this Spirit.

The lesson Jesus teaches us today in His school is this: that the Father is just longing to give Him to us if we will but ask in the childlike dependence on what He says: "If ye . . . know how to give good gifts unto your children, how much more shall your heavenly Father give the Holy Spirit to them that ask him." In the words of God's promise, "I will pour out my Spirit *abundantly*"; and of His command, "Be ye *filled* with the Spirit," we have the measure of what God is ready to give, and what we may obtain. As God's children, we have already received the Spirit. But we still need to ask and pray for His special gifts and operations as we require them. And not only this, but for the Spirit to take complete and entire possession and for His unceasing momentary guidance. Just as the branch, already filled with the sap of the vine, is always crying for the continued and increasing flow of that sap, that it may bring its fruit to perfection, so the believer, rejoicing in the possession of the Spirit, ever thirsts and cries for more. And what the great Teacher would have us learn is that nothing less than God's promise and God's command may be the measure of our expectation and our prayer; we must be filled abundantly. He would have us ask this in the assurance that the wonderful how much more of God's Father-love is the pledge that, when we ask, we do certainly receive.

Let us now believe this. As we pray to be filled with the Spirit, let us not seek for the answer in our feelings. All spiritual blessings must be received, that is, accepted or taken in faith.[1] Let us believe that the Father *gives* the Holy Spirit to His praying child. Even now, while we pray, we must say in faith: I have what I ask, the fullness of the Spirit is mine. Let us continue steadfast in this faith. On the strength of God's Word we know that we have what we ask. Let us, with thanksgiving that we have been heard, with thanksgiving for what we have received and taken and now hold as ours, continue steadfast in believing prayer that the blessing, *which has already been given us,* and which we hold in faith, may break through and fill our whole being. It is in such believing thanksgiving and prayer that our soul opens up for the Spirit to take entire and undisturbed possession. It is such prayer that not only asks and hopes, but takes and holds, that inherits the full blessing. In all our prayer let us remember the lesson the Savior would teach us this day that, *if there is there is one thing on earth we can be sure of, it is this, that the Father desires to have us filled with His Spirit and that He delights to give us His Spirit.*

When once we have learned to believe for ourselves, and each day to take out of the treasure we hold in heaven, what liberty and power we have to pray for the outpouring of the Spirit on the church of God, on all flesh, on individuals, or on special efforts! He who has once learned to know the Father in prayer for himself, learns to pray most confidently for

[1]The Greek word for receiving and taking is the same. When Jesus said, "Every one that asketh, *receiveth,*" He used the same verb as at the Supper, "*Take,* eat," or on the resurrection morning, "*Receive,*" accept, take, "the Holy Spirit." Receiving not only implies God's bestowment, but our acceptance.

others too. The Father gives the Holy Spirit to those who ask Him, not least, but most, when they ask for others.

* * * * *

Father in heaven, You did send Your Son to reveal Yourself to us, Your Father-love, and all that that love has for us. And He has taught us that the gift above all gifts that You would bestow in answer to prayer is the Holy Spirit.

O my Father, I come to You with this prayer: there is nothing I would—may I not say, I do—desire so much as to be filled with the Spirit, the Holy Spirit. The blessings He brings are so unspeakable, and just what I need. He sheds abroad Your love in the heart, and fills it with Yourself. I long for this. He breathes the mind and life of Christ in me, so that I live as He did, in and for the Father's love. I long for this. He endues with power from on high for all my walk and work. I long for this. I beseech You O Father!, give me this day the fullness of Thy Spirit.

Father, I ask this, resting on the words of my Lord: "how much more the Holy Spirit." I do believe that You hear my prayer; I receive now what I ask; Father! I claim and I take it: the fullness of Your Spirit as mine. I receive the gift this day again as a faith gift; in faith I consider my Father works through the Spirit all He has promised. The Father delights to breathe His Spirit into His waiting child as He tarries in fellowship with Himself. Amen.

8 The Boldness of God's Friends

And he said unto them, Which of you shall have a friend, and shall go in unto him at midnight, and say to him, Friend, lend me three loaves; for a friend of mine is come to me from a journey, and I have nothing to set before him; and he from within shall answer and say, Trouble me not: the door is now shut, and my children are with me in bed; I cannot rise and give thee? I say unto you, though he will not rise and give him because he is his friend, yet because of his importunity he will rise and give him as many as he needeth.

Luke 11:5-8

The first teaching by our Lord to His disciples was given in the Sermon on the Mount. It was almost a year later that the disciples asked Jesus to teach them to pray. In answer He gave them the Lord's Prayer a second time, so teaching them *what* to pray. He then speaks of *how* they ought to pray, and repeats what he formerly said of God's fatherliness and the certainty of an answer. But in between He adds the beautiful parable of the friend at midnight, to teach them the twofold lesson, that God not only wants us to pray for ourselves, but for the perishing around us, and that in such intercession great boldness of request is often needful, and always lawful, yea, pleasing to God.

The parable is a perfect storehouse of instruction in regard to true intercession. There is first *the love* that seeks to help the needy around us: "*my friend* is come to me." Then *the need* that the cry expresses: "*I have nothing* to set before him". Then follows *the confidence* that help is to be had:

which of you shall have a *friend,* and say, "*Friend,* lend me three loaves." Then comes the unexpected *refusal*; "I *cannot* rise and give thee." Then again the *perseverance* that takes no refusal: "because of his *importunity.*" And lastly, the reward of such prayer: "he will . . . give him *as many as he needeth.*" This is a wonderful setting forth of the way of prayer and faith in which the blessing of God has so often been sought and found.

Let us confine ourselves to the chief thought that prayer is an appeal to the friendship of God, and we shall find that two lessons are especially suggested. The one, that if we are God's friends, and come as such to Him, we must prove ourselves the friends of the needy; God's friendship to us and ours to others go hand in hand. The other, that when we come in this way we may use the utmost liberty in claiming an answer.

There is a twofold use of prayer: the one, to obtain strength and blessing for our own life; the other, the higher, the true glory of prayer, for which Christ has taken us into His fellowship and teaching, is intercession, where prayer is the royal power a child of God exercises in heaven on behalf of others and even of the kingdom. We see in Scripture how it was in intercession for others that Abraham and Moses, Samuel and Elijah, with all the holy men of old, proved that they had power with God and prevailed. It is when we give ourselves to be a blessing that we can especially count on the blessing of God. It is when we draw near to God as the friend of the poor and the perishing that we may count on His friendliness; the righteous man who is the friend of the poor is in a special way the friend of God. This gives wonderful liberty in prayer. Lord, I have a needy friend whom I must help. As a friend I have undertaken to help him. In You I have a Friend, whose kindness and riches I know to be infinite: I am sure You will give what I ask. If I, being evil, am ready to do for my friend what I can, how much more will You, O my heavenly Friend, now do for Your friend what he asks?

The question itself might suggest whether the fatherhood of God does not give such confidence in prayer, that the thought of His friendship can hardly teach us anything more: a father is more than a friend. And yet, if we consider it, this pleading the friendship of God opens new wonders to us. That a child receives what he asks of his father looks so perfectly natural that we almost count it the father's duty to give. But with a friend it is as if the kindness is more free, dependent, not on nature, but on sympathy and character. And then the relation of a child is more that of perfect dependence; two friends are more nearly on a level. So our Lord, in seeking to unfold to us the spiritiual mystery of prayer, would have us approach God in this relation too, as those whom He has acknowledged as His friends, whose mind and life are in sympathy with His.

But then we must be living as His friends. I am still a child even when a wanderer; but friendship depends on the conduct. "Ye are my friends, if ye do the things which I command you." "Thou seest that faith wrought with his works, and by works was faith made perfect; and the scripture was fulfilled which saith, And Abraham believed God . . . and he was called *the friend of God*." It is the Spirit, "*the same* Spirit," that leads us that also bears witness to our acceptance with God; "*likewise,* also," the same Spirit helps us in prayer. It is a life as the friend of God that gives the wonderful liberty to say: I have a friend to whom I can go even at midnight. And how much more when I go in the very spirit of that friendliness manifesting myself the very kindness I look for in God, seeking to help my friend as I want God to help me. When I come to God in prayer, He always looks at the aim of my petition. If it is merely for my own comfort or joy that I seek His grace, I do not receive. But if I can say that it is that He may be glorified in my dispensing His blessings to others, I shall not ask in vain. Or if I ask for others, but want to wait until God has made me so rich that it is no sacrifice or act of faith to aid them, I shall not receive. But if I can say that I have already undertaken for my needy friend, that in my poverty I have already begun the work of love, because I know I had a friend who would help me, my prayer will be heard. Oh, we know not how much the plea avails: the friendship of earth looking in its need to the friendship of heaven: "He will give him as much as he needeth."

But not always at once. The one thing by which man can

honor and enjoy his God is *faith.* Intercession is part of faith's training school. There our friendship with man and with God is tested. There it is seen whether my friendship with the needy is so real that I will take time and sacrifice my rest, will go even at midnight and not cease until I have obtained for them what I need. There it is seen whether my friendship with God is so clear that I can depend on Him not to turn me away and therefore pray on until He gives.

What a deep heavenly mystery this is of persevering prayer. The God who has promised, who longs, whose fixed purpose it is to give the blessing, holds it back. It is to Him a matter of such deep importance that His friends on earth should know and fully trust their rich Friend in heaven, that He trains them in the school of answer delayed, to find out how their perseverance really does prevail, and what the mighty power is they can wield in heaven, if they do but set themselves to it. There is a faith that sees the promise, and embraces it, and yet does not receive it (Heb. 11:13, 39). It is when the answer to prayer does not come, and the promise we are most firmly trusting appears to be of no effect, that the trial of faith, more precious than of gold, takes place. It is in this trial that the faith that has embraced the promise is purified and strengthened and prepared in personal, holy fellowship with the living God, to see the glory of God. It takes and holds the promise until it has received the fulfillment of what it had claimed in a living truth in the unseen but living God.

Let each child of God who is seeking to work the work of love in his Father's service take courage. The parent with his child, the teacher with his class, the visitor with his district, the Bible reader with his circle, the preacher with his hearers, each one who, in his little circle, has accepted and is bearing the burden of hungry, perishing souls—let them all take courage. Nothing is at first so strange to us as that God should really require persevering prayer, that there should be a real spiritual needs be for importunity. To teach it to us, the Master uses this almost strange parable. If the unfriendliness of a selfish earthly friend can be conquered by persistance, how much more will it avail with the heavenly Friend, who does so love to give, but is held back by our spiritual unfitness, our incapacity to possess what He has to give. Let us thank Him that in delaying His answer He is educating us to our true position and the exercise of all our power with Him, training us to live with Him in the fellowship of undoubting faith and trust, to be indeed the friends of God. And let us hold fast the threefold cord that cannot be broken: the hungry friend needing the help, the praying friend seeking the help, and the mighty Friend, loving to give as much as His friend needs.

* * * * *

O my blessed Lord and Teacher, I must come to You in prayer. Your teaching is so glorious, and yet too high for me to grasp. I must confess that my heart is too little to take in these thoughts of the wonderful boldness I may use with Your Father as my Friend. Lord Jesus, I trust You to give me Your Spirit with Your Word, and to make the Word quick and powerful in my heart. I desire to keep Your word of this day: "Because of his importunity he will rise and give him as many as he needeth."

Lord, teach me to know more of the power of persevering prayer. I know that in it the Father suits Himself to our need of time for the inner life to attain its growth and ripeness, so that His grace may indeed be assimilated and made our own. I know that He desires to train us to the exercise of that strong faith that does not let Him go even in the face of seeming disappointment. I know He wants to lift us to that wonderful liberty, in which we understand how really He has made the dispensing of His gift dependent on our prayer. I know this Lord, teach me to see it in spirit and truth.

And may it now be the joy of my life to become the distributor of my rich Friend in heaven, to care for all the hungry and perishing, even at midnight, because I know my Friend, who always gives to him who perseveres, because of his entreating, as much as he needs. Amen.

9 *Prayer Provides Laborers*

Then saith he unto his disciples, The harvest indeed is plen-
teous, but the laborers are few. Pray ye therefore the Lord
of the harvest, that he send forth laborers into his harvest.
Matthew 9:37-38

The Lord frequently taught His disciples *that* they must pray,
and *how*; but seldom *what* to pray. This He left to their sense
of need, and the leading of the Spirit. But here we have one
thing He expressly enjoins them to remember: in view of the
plenteous harvest, and the need of reapers, they must cry to
the Lord of the harvest to send forth laborers. Just as in the
parable of the friend at midnight, He would have them understand that prayer is not to be selfish; here also it is the power
through which blessing can come to others. The Father is
Lord of the harvest; when we pray for the Holy Spirit, we must
pray for Him to prepare and send forth laborers for the work.

Strange, is it not, that He should ask His disciples to pray
for this? And could He not pray Himself? Would not one of
His prayers avail more than a thousand of theirs? And God,
the Lord of the harvest, did He not see the need? And would
He, in His own good time, send forth laborers without their
prayer? Such questions lead us up to the deepest mysteries
of prayer, and its power in the kingdom of God. The answer
to such questions will convince us that prayer is indeed a
power on which the ingathering of the harvest and the coming of the kingdom do in truth depend.

Prayer is no form or show. The Lord Jesus was Himself the
truth; everything He spake was the deepest truth. It was when
"He saw the multitudes, he was moved with compassion for

them, because they were distressed and scattered as sheep not having a shepherd," that He called on the disciples to pray for laborers to be sent among them. He did so because He really believed that their prayer was needed, and would help. The veil that so hides the invisible world from us was wonderfully transparent to the holy human soul of Jesus. He had looked long and deep and far into the hidden connection of cause and effect in the spirit world. He had marked in God's Word how, when God called men like Abraham and Moses, Joshua and Samuel and Daniel, and given them authority over men in His name, He had at the same time given them authority and right to call on the powers of heaven for aid as they needed them. He knew that as to these men of old, and to Himself for a time here upon earth, the work of God had been entrusted, so it was now about to pass into the hands of His disciples. He knew that when this work should be given in charge to them, it would not be a mere matter of form or show, but that on them, and their being faithful or unfaithful, the success of the work would actually depend. As a single individual, within the limitations of a human body and a human life, Jesus feels how little a short visit can accomplish among these wandering sheep He sees around Him, and He longs for help to have them properly cared for. So He tells His disciples now to begin to pray and, when they have taken over the work from Him on earth, to make this one of the chief petitions in their prayer: that the Lord of the harvest Himself would send forth laborers into His harvest. The God who entrusted them with the work, and made it largely to depend on them, gives them the authority to apply to Him for laborers to help, and makes the supply dependent on their prayer.

How little do Christians really feel and mourn the need of laborers in the fields of the world so white to the harvest. And how little they believe that our labor supply depends on prayer, that prayer will really provide "as many as he needeth." It is not that the dearth of labor is not known or discussed; not that efforts are not sometimes put forth to supply the want. He is concerned about how little the burden of the sheep wandering without a Shepherd is really borne in the faith that the Lord of the harvest *will*, in answer to prayer, send forth the laborers, and in the solemn conviction that without this prayer fields ready for reaping will be left to perish. It is still so. So wonderful is the surrender of His work into the hands of His church, so dependent has the Lord made Himself on them as His body, through whom alone His work can be done, so real is the power that the Lord gives His people to exercise in heaven and earth, that the number of the laborers and the measure of the harvest actually depends on their prayers.

Solemn thought! Why is it that we do not obey the injunction of the Master more heartily, and cry more earnestly for laborers? There are two reasons for this. The one is that we miss the compassion of Jesus, which gave rise to this request for prayer. When believers learn that to love their neighbors as themselves, that to live entirely for God's glory in their fellowmen, is the Father's first commandment to His redeemed ones, they will accept the charge of the perishing entrusted to them by their Lord. And, accepting them not only as a field of labor, but as the objects of loving care and interest, it will not be long before compassion toward the hopelessly perishing will touch their heart, and the cry ascend with an earnestness till then unknown: Lord! send laborers. The other reason for the neglect of the command, the want of faith, will then make itself felt, but will be overcome as our pity pleads for help. We believe too little in the power of prayer to bring about definite results. We do not live close enough to God, and are not entriely given up to His service and kingdom, to be capable of the confidence that He will give it in answer to our prayer. O let us pray for a life so one with Christ, that His compassion may stream into us, and His Spirit be able to assure us that our prayer avails.

Such prayer will ask for and receive a twofold blessing. There will first be the desire for the increase of people entirely given up to the service of God. It is a terrible blot on the church of Christ that there are times when actually people cannot be found for the service of the Master as ministers, missionaries, or teachers of God's Word. As God's children make this a matter of supplication for their own circle or church, it will be given. The Lord Jesus is now Lord of the harvest. He has been exalted to bestow gifts—the gifts of the

Spirit. His chief gifts are men filled with the Spirit. But the supply and distribution of the gifts depend on the cooperation of Head and members. It is just prayer that will lead to such cooperation; the believing suppliants will be stirred to find the workers and the means for the work.

The other blessing to be asked will not be less. Every believer is a laborer; not one of God's children who has not been redeemed for service, and then has no work waiting. It must be our prayer that the Lord would so fill all His people with the spirit of devotion that not one may be found standing idle in the vineyard. Wherever there is a complaint of lack of helpers, or of fit helpers in God's work, prayer has the promise of a supply. There is no Sunday school or district calling, no Bible reading or rescue work, where God is not ready and able to provide. It may take time and persistence, but the command of Christ to ask the Lord of the harvest is the pledge that the prayer will be heard: "I say unto you, he will airse and give him as many as he needeth."

Solemn, blessed thought! This power has been given us in prayer to provide, in the need of the world, servants for God's work. The Lord of the harvest will hear. Christ, who called us so specifically to pray thus, will support our prayers offered in His name and interest. Let us set apart time and give ourselves to this part of our intercessory work. It will lead us into the fellowship of that compassionate heart of His that led Him to call for our prayers. It will elevate us to the insight of our regal position, as those whose will counts for something with the great God in the advancement of His kingdom. It will make us feel how truly we are God's fellow workers on earth, to whom a share in His work has been entrusted. It will make us partakers in the soul travail, but also in the soul satisfaction of Jesus, as we know how, in answer to our prayer, blessing has been given that otherwise would not have come.

*   *   *   *   *

Blessed Lord! You have this day again given us another of Your wondrous lessons to learn. We humbly ask You, O give us to see aright the spiritual realities of which You have been speaking. There is the harvest that is so large and perishing, as it waits for sleepy disciples to give the signal for laborers to come. Lord, teach us to look out on it with a heart moved with compassion and pity. There are the laborers, so few. Lord, show us how terrible the sin of the want of prayer and faith, of which this is the token. And there is the Lord of the harvest, so able and ready to send them forth. Lord, show us how He does indeed wait for the prayer to which He has bound His answer. And there are the disciples, to whom the commission to pray has been given: Lord, show us how You can pour down Your Spirit and breathe on them, so that Your compassion and the faith in Your promise shall rouse them to unceasing, prevailing prayer.

O our Lord, we cannot understand how You can entrust such work and give such power to men so slothful and unfaithful. We thank You for all whom You are teaching to cry day and night for laborers to be sent forth. Lord, breathe Your own Spirit on all Your children, that they may learn to live for this one thing alone—the kingdom and glory of their Lord—and become fully awake to the faith of what their prayer can accomplish. And let all our hearts in this, as in every petition, be filled with the assurance that prayer, offered in loving faith in the living God, will bring certain and abundant answer. Amen.

10 Prayer Must Be Definite

And Jesus answered him, and said, What wilt thou that I should do unto thee?

Mark 10:51; Luke 18:41

The blind man had been crying out, and frequently, "Thou Son of David, have mercy on me." The cry had reached the ear of the Lord; He knew what he wanted, and was ready to grant it to him. But before He does it, He asks him: "*What wilt thou* that I should do unto thee?" He wants to hear from the blind man's own lips, not only the general petition for mercy, but also the distinct expression of what his desire was. Until he speaks it out, he is not healed.

There is now still many a suppliant to whom the Lord puts the same question, and who cannot, until it has been answered, get the aid he or she asks. Our prayers must not be a vague appeal to His mercy, an infinite cry for blessing, but the distinct expression of definite need. It is not that His loving heart does not understand our cry, or is not ready to hear. But He desires it for our own sakes. Such definite prayer teaches us to know our own needs better. It demands time, and thought, and self-scrutiny to find out what really is our greatest need. It searches us and puts us to the test as to whether our desires are honest and real, such as we are ready to persevere in. It leads us to judge whether our desires are according to God's Word, and whether we really believe that we shall receive the things we ask. It helps us to wait for the special answer, and to mark it when it comes.

And yet how much of our prayer is vague and pointless. Some cry for mercy, but do not take the trouble to know what mercy must do for them. Others ask, perhaps, to be delivered of sin, but do not begin by bringing any sin by name from which the deliverance may be claimed. Still others pray for God's blessing on those around them, for the outpouring of God's Spirit on their land or the world, and yet have no special field where they wait and expect to see the answer. To all the Lord says: And now what is it you really want and expect Me to do? Every Christian has but limited powers, and as he must have his own special field of labor in which he works, so with his prayers too. Each believer has his own circle, his family, his friends, his neighbors. If he were to mention one or more of these by name, he would find that this brings him into the training school of faith, and leads to personal and pointed dealing with his God. It is when in such distinct matters we have in faith claimed and received answers, that our more general prayers will be believing and effectual.

In hunting game the hunter has learned a different lesson: his practiced eye sends every bullet on its special message, to seek and find its target. Such aiming must gain the day in the spiritual world too. If in prayer we just pour out our hearts in a multitude of petitions, without taking time to see whether every petition is sent with the purpose and expectation of getting an answer, not many will reach the mark. But if, as in silence of soul we bow before the Lord, we were to ask such questions as these: What is now really my desire? Do I desire it in faith, expecting to receive? Am I now ready to place and leave it in the Father's bosom? Is it a settled thing between God and me that I am to have the answer? We would learn to pray so that God would see our need and we would know what to really expect.

It is for this, among other reasons, that the Lord warns us against the vain repetitions of the Gentiles, who think they were heard because they prayed much. We often hear prayers of great earnestness and fervor, in which a multitude of petitions are pored forth, but to which the Savior would undoubtedly answer, 'What wilt thou that I should do unto thee?' If I am in a strange land, in the interests of the business that my father owns, I would certainly write two different sorts of letters. There would be family letters giving expression to all the intercourse to which affection prompts; and there would be business letters, containing orders for what I need. And there may be letters in which both are found. The answers will correspond to the letters. To each sentence of the letters containing the family news I do not expect a special answer. But for each order I send I am confident of an answer whether or not the desired article has been forwarded. In our dealings with God the business element must not be wanting. With our expression of need and sin, of love and faith and consecration, there must be the pointed statement of what we ask and expect to receive; the answer that the Father loves to give us is the token of His approval and acceptance.

But the word of the Master teaches us more. He does not say, What do you *wish*? but, What do you *will*? We may often wish for a thing without willing it. I wish to have a certain article, but I find the price too high; I resolve not to take it; I *wish*, but do not *will* to have it. The sluggard wishes to be rich, but does not will it. Many people wish to be saved, but perish because they do not will it. The will rules the whole heart and life; if I really will to have anything that is within my reach, I do not rest until I have it. And so, when Jesus says to us, "What do you will?" He asks whether it is indeed our purpose to have what we ask at any price, however great the sacrifice. Do you indeed so will to have it that, although He delays it, do you not hold your peace until He hear you? Alas! how many prayers are wishes, sent up for a short time and then forgotten, or sent up year after year as a matter of duty, while we rest content with the prayer without the answer.

But, it may be asked, is it not best to make our wishes known to God, and then to leave it to Him to decide what is best, without seeking to assert our will? By no means. This is the very essence of the prayer of faith, to which Jesus sought to train His disciples, that it does not only make known its desire and then leave the decision to God. That would be the prayer of submission, for cases in which we cannot know God's will. But the prayer of faith, finding God's will in some promise of the Word, pleads for that until it comes. In Matthew (9:28) we read that Jesus said to the blind man: "*Believe ye* that I am able to do this?" Here, in Mark, He says: "*What wilt thou* that I should do?" In both cases He said that faith had saved them. And He also said to the Syrophenician woman: "Great is thy *faith*: be it unto thee even as thou *wilt.*" Faith is nothing but the purpose of the will resting on God's word, and saying: I must have it. To believe truly is to will firmly.

But is not such a will at variance with our dependence on God and our submission to Him? By no means; it is much rather the true submission that honors God. It is only when the child has yielded his own will in entire surrender to the Father that he receives from the Father liberty and power to will what he would have. But, when once the believer has accepted the will of God, as revealed through the Word and Spirit, as his will, too, then it is the will of God that His child should use this renewed will in His service. The will is the highest power in the soul; grace wants above everything to sanctify and restore this will, one of the chief traits of God's image, to full and free exercise. As a son, who only lives for his father's interests, who seeks not his own but his father's will, is trusted by the father with his business, so God speaks to His child in all truth, "What will you?" It is often spiritual sloth that, under the appearance of humility, professes to have no will, because it fears the trouble of searching out the will of God or, when found, the struggle of claiming it in faith. True humility is ever in company with strong faith, which only seeks to know what is according to the will of God, and then boldly claims the fulfillment of the promise: "Ye shall ask *what ye will,* and it shall be done unto you."

* * * * *

Lord Jesus! teach me to pray with all my heart and strength, that there may be no doubt with You or with me as to what I have asked. May I so know what I desire that, even as my petitions are recorded in heaven, I can record them on earth too, and note each answer as it comes. And may my faith in what Your Word has promised be so clear that the Spirit may indeed work in me the liberty to will that it shall come. Lord, renew, strengthen, sanctify wholly my will for the work of effectual prayer.

Blessed Savior! I do beg You to reveal to me the wonderful condescension You show us, thus asking us to say what we will that You should do, and promising to do whatever we will. Son of God! I cannot understand it; I can only say I believe that You have indeed redeemed us wholly for Yourself, and seek to make the will, as our noblest part, Your most efficient servant. Lord! I do most unreservedly yield my will to You, as the power through which Your Spirit is to rule my whole being. Let Him take possession of it, lead it into the truth of Your promises, and make it so strong in prayer that I may ever hear Your voice saying: "Great is thy faith: be it unto thee even as thou wilt." Amen.

11 *The Faith That Takes*

Therefore I say unto you, All things whatsoever ye pray and ask for, believe that ye receive them, and ye shall have them.

Mark 11:24

What a promise! so large, so divine, that our little hearts cannot take it in, and in every possible way seek to limit it to what we think safe or probable; instead of allowing it, in its quickening power and energy, just as He gave it, to enter in, and to enlarge our hearts to the measure of what His love and power are really ready to do for us. Faith is far from being a mere conviction of the truth of God's word, or a conclusion drawn from certain premises. It is the ear that has heard God say what He will do, the eye that has seen Him doing it, and, therefore, where there is true faith, the answer must come. If we only see to it that we do the one thing that He asks of us as we pray: Believe *that ye receive*; He will see to it that He does the thing He has promised: *"Ye shall have them."* The keynote of Solomon's prayer (2 Chron. 6:4), "Blessed be the Lord God of Israel, who . . . hath *with his hands fulfilled* that which *He spoke with his mouth* to my father David," is the keynote of all true prayer: the joyful adoration of a God whose *hand* always secures the fulfillment of what His *mouth* has spoken. Let us in this spirit listen to the promise Jesus gives; each part of it has its divine message.

"All things whatsoever." At this first word our human wisdom at once begins to doubt and ask: This surely cannot be literally true? But if it is not, why did the Master speak it, using the strongest expression He could find: "All things

whatsoever." And it is not as if this were the only time He spoke this way; is it not He who also said, "If thou canst believe, all things are possible to him that believeth"; "If ye have faith, nothing shall be impossible to you." Faith is so wholly the work of God's Spirit through His word in the prepared heart of the believing disciple, that it is impossible that the fulfillment should not come; faith is the pledge and forerunner of the coming answer. Yes, "all things whatsoever ye shall ask in prayer *believing, ye receive.*" The tendency of human reason is to interpose here, and with certain qualifying clauses, "if expedient," "if according to God's will," to break the force of a statement that appears dangerous. Let us beware of dealing with the Master's words in this way. His promise is most literally true. He wants His oft-repeated "all things" to enter into our hearts, and reveal to us how mighty the power of faith is, how truly the Head calls the members to share with Him in His power, how wholly our Father places His power at the disposal of the child who wholly trusts Him. In this "all things" faith is to have its food and strength: as we weaken it we weaken faith. The "whatsoever" is unconditional: the only condition is what is implied in the believing. Before we can believe we must find out and know what God's will is; believing is the exercise of a soul surrendered and given up to the influence of the Word and the Spirit; but when once we believe nothing would be impossible. God forbid that we should try and bring down His "all things" to the level of what we think possible. Let us now simply take Christ's "whatsoever" as the measure and the hope of our faith: it is a seed word which, if taken just as He gives it, and kept in the heart, will unfold itself and strike root, fill our life with its fullness, and bring forth fruit abundantly.

"All things whatsoever *ye pray and ask for.*" It is in prayer that these "all things" are to be brought to God, to be asked and received of Him. The faith that receives them is the fruit of the prayer. In one aspect there must be faith before there can be prayer; in another the faith is the outcome and the growth of prayer. It is in the personal presence of the Savior, in intercourse with Him, that faith rises to grasp what at first appeared too high. It is in prayer that we hold up our desire to the light of God's holy will, that our motives are tested, and proof given whether we ask indeed in the name of Jesus, and only for the glory of God. It is in prayer that we wait for the leading of the Spirit to show us whether we are asking the right thing and in the right spirit. It is in prayer that we become conscious of our want of faith, that we are led on to say to the Father that we do believe, and that we prove the reality of our faith by the confidence with which we persevere. It is in prayer that Jesus teaches and inspires faith. He who waits to pray, or loses heart in prayer, because he does not feel the faith needed to get the answer, will never learn to believe. He who begins to pray and ask will find that the Spirit of faith is given nowhere so surely as at the foot of the throne.

"*Believe* that ye receive." It is clear that what we are to believe is that we receive the very things we ask. The Savior does not hint that because the Father knows what is best He may give us something else. The very mountain faith bids depart is cast into the sea. There is a prayer in which, in everything, we make known our requests with prayer and supplication, and the reward is the sweet peace of God keeping heart and mind. This is the prayer of trust. It has reference to things of which we cannot find out if God is going to give them. As children we make known our desires in the countless things of daily life, and leave it to the Father to give or not as He thinks best. But the prayer of faith of which Jesus speaks is something different, something higher. When, whether in the greater interests of the Master's work, or in the lesser concerns of our daily life, the soul is led to see how there is nothing that so honors the Father as the faith that is assured that He will do what He has said in giving us whatsoever we ask for, and takes its stand on the promise as brought home by the Spirit, it may know most certainly that it does receive exactly what it asks. Just see how clearly the Lord sets this before us in verse 23: "Whosoever . . . shall not doubt in his heart, but shall believe that *what he saith* cometh to pass; he shall have it." This is the blessing of the prayer of faith of which Jesus speaks.

"Believe that ye *receive.*" This is the word of central importance, of which the meaning is too often misunderstood. Believe that you have received, now, while praying, the thing you ask for. It may only be later that you shall have it in personal experience, that you shall see what you believe; but now, without seeing, you are to believe that it has been given you of the Father in heaven. The receiving or accepting of an answer to prayer is just like the receiving or accepting of Jesus or of pardon, a spiritual thing, an act of faith apart from all feeling. When I come as a supplicant for pardon, I believe that Jesus in heaven is for me, so I receive or take Him. When I come as a supplicant for any special gift, which is according to Gods Word, I believe that what I ask is given me: I believe that I have it, I hold it in faith; I thank God that it is mine. "If we know that he heareth us whatsoever we ask, we know that we have the petitions which we have asked of him."

"And ye shall have them." That is, the gift that we first hold in faith as bestowed on us in heaven will also become ours in personal experience. But will it be needful to pray longer if once we know we have been heard and have received what we asked? There are cases in which such prayer will not be needful, in which the blessing is ready to break through at once, if we but hold fast our confidence, and prove our faith by praising God for what we have received, in the face of our not yet having it in experience. There are other cases in which the faith that has received needs to be still further tried and strengthened in persevering prayer. God only knows when everything in and around us is fully ripe for the manifestation of the blessing that has been given in faith. Elijah knew for certain that rain would come; God had promised it; and yet he had to pray seven times. And that prayer was no show or play; it was an intense spiritual reality in the heart of him who lay pleading there, and in the heaven above where it had its effectual work to do. It is "through faith *and patience* we inherit the promises." Faith says most confidently, I have received it. Patience perseveres in prayer until the gift bestowed in heaven is seen on earth. "Believe that *ye have received,* and *ye shall have.*" Between the *have received* in heaven, and the *shall have* of earth, *believe*; believing praise and prayer is the link.

And now, remember one thing more: It is Jesus who said this. As we see heaven opened to us in this way, and the Father on the throne offering to give us whatever we ask in faith, our hearts feel full of shame that we have so little availed ourselves of our privilege, and full of fear lest our feeble faith still fails to grasp what is so clearly placed within our reach. There is one thing that must make us strong and full of hope: it is Jesus who has brought us this message from the Father. He Himself, when He was on earth, lived the life of faith and prayer. It was when the disciples expressed their surprise at what He had done to the fig tree, that He told them that the same life He led could be theirs; that they could not command only the fig tree, but the very mountain, and it must obey. And He is our life: all He was on earth He is in us now; all He teaches He really gives. He is Himself the Author and the Perfecter of our faith. He gives the spirit of faith; let us not be afraid that such faith is not meant for us. It is meant for every child of the Father; it is within reach of each one who will but be childlike, yielding himself to the Father's will and love, trusting the Father's word and power. Dear fellow Christian, let the thought that this word comes through Jesus, the Son, our Brother, give us courage, and let our answer be: Yes, blessed Lord, we do believe Your Word, we do believe that we receive.

*　*　*　*　*

Blessed Lord! You came from the Father to show us all His Love, and all the treasures of blessing that love is waiting to bestow. Lord, You have this day again flung the gates so wide open, and given us such promises as to our liberty in prayer, that we must blush that our poor hearts have so little taken it in. It has been too large for us to believe.

We now look up to You to teach us to take and keep and use this precious word of Yours: "All things whatsoever ye ask, believe that ye receive." Blessed Jesus! it is You in whom our faith must be rooted if it is to grow strong. Your work has freed us wholly from the power of sin, and opened the way to the Father; Your love is ever longing to bring us into the full fellowship of Your glory and power; Your Spirit is ever drawing us upward into a life of perfect faith and confidence; we are assured that in Your teaching we shall learn to pray the prayer of faith. You will train us to pray so that we believe that we receive, to believe that we really have what we ask. Lord, teach me so to know and trust and love You, so to live and abide in You, that all my prayers rise up and come before God in You, and that my soul may have in You the assurance that I am heard. Amen.

12 The Secret of Believing Prayer

Jesus answering saith unto them, Have faith in God. Verily I say unto you, Whosoever . . . shall not doubt in his heart, but shall believe that what he saith cometh to pass; he shall have it. Therefore I say unto you, All things whatsoever ye pray and ask for, believe that ye receive them, and ye shall have them.

Mark 11:22-24

The promise of answer to prayer that formed the last chapter is one of the most wonderful in all Scripture. In many hearts it has raised the question: How can I ever attain the faith that knows that it receives all it asks?

It is this question our Lord would answer now. Before He gave that wonderful promise to His disciples, He spoke another word, in which He pointed out where the faith in the answer to prayer comes from, and ever finds its strength. Have faith in God. This word precedes the other: have faith in the promise of an answer to prayer. The power to believe *a promise* depends entirely, but only, on faith in *the promiser.* Trust in the person begets trust in his word. It is only where we live and associate with God in personal, loving intercourse, where God Himself is all to us, where our whole being is continually opened up and exposed to the mighty influences that are at work where His holy presence is revealed, that the capacity will be developed for believing that He gives whatever we ask for.

This connection between faith in God and faith in His promise will become clear to us if we understand what faith really is. It is often compared to the hand or the mouth by which we take and appropriate what is offered to us. But it is of importance that we should understand that faith is also the ear by which I hear what is promised, the eye by which I see what is offered me. On this the power to take depends. I must *hear* the person who gives me the promise: the very tone of his voice gives me courage to believe. I must *see* him: in the light of his eye and countenance all fear as to my right to take passes away. The value of the promise depends on the promiser: it is on my knowledge of what the promiser is that faith in the promise depends.

It is for this reason that Jesus, before He gives that wonderful prayer promise, first says, "Have Faith in God." That is, let your eye be open to the living God, and gaze on Him, seeing Him who is invisible. It is through the eye that I yield myself to the influence of what is before me; I just allow it to enter, to exert its influence, to leave its impression on my mind. So believing God is just looking to God and what He is, allowing Him to reveal His presence, giving Him time and yielding the whole being to take in the full impression of what He is as God, the soul opened up to receive and rejoice in the overshadowing of His love. Yes, faith is the eye to which God shows what He is and does: through faith the light of His presence and the workings of His mighty power stream into the soul. As that which I see lives in me, so by faith God lives in me too.

And even so faith is also the ear through which the voice of God is always heard and intercourse with Him kept up. It is through the Holy Spirit the Father speaks to us; the Son is the Word, the substance of what God says; the Spirit is the living voice. This the child of God needs to lead and guide him; the secret voice from heaven must teach him, as it taught Jesus what to say and what to do. An ear opened toward God, that is, a believing heart waiting on Him, to hear what He says, will hear Him speak. The words of God will not only be the words of a Book, but, proceeding from the mouth of God, they will be spirit and truth, life and power. They will bring in deed and living experience what are otherwise only thoughts. Through this opened ear the soul tarries under the influence of the life and power of God Himself. As the words

I hear enter the mind and dwell and work there, so through faith God enters the heart, and dwells and works there.

When faith now is in full exercise as eye and ear, as the faculty of the soul by which we see and hear God, then it will be able to exercise its full power as hand and mouth, by which we appropriate God and His blessings. The power of reception will depend entirely on the power of spiritual perception. For this reason Jesus said, before He gave the promise that God would answer believing prayer: "Have Faith in God." Faith is simply surrender: I yield myself to the impression the tidings I hear make on me. By faith *I yield myself to the living God.* His glory and love fill my heart, and have the mastery over my life. Faith is fellowship; I give myself up to the influence of the friend who makes me a promise, and become linked to him by it. And it is when we enter into this living fellowship *with God Himself,* in a faith that always sees and hears Him, that it becomes easy and natural to believe His promise as to prayer. Faith in the promise is the fruit of faith in the promiser: the prayer of faith is rooted in the life of faith. And in this way the faith that prays effectually is indeed a gift of God. Not as something that He bestows or infuses at once, but in a far deeper and truer sense, as the blessed disposition or habit of soul that developed and grows up in us in a life of intercourse with Him. Surely for one who knows his Father well, and lives in constant close intercourse with Him, it is a simple thing to believe the promise that He will do the will of His child who lives in union with Himself.

It is because many of God's children do not understand this connection between the life of faith and the prayer of faith that their experience of the power of prayer is so limited. When they desire earnestly to obtain an answer from God, they fix their whole heart on the promise, and try their utmost to grasp that promise in faith. When they do not succeed, they are ready to give up hope; the promise is true, but it is beyond their power to take hold of it in faith. Listen to the lesson Jesus teaches us this day: Have faith in God, the living God. Let faith look to God more than the thing promised: His love, His power, His living presence will waken and work the faith. A physician would say to someone asking how he can get more strength in his arms and hands to seize and hold, that his whole constitution must be built up and strengthened. So the cure of a feeble faith is alone to be found in the invigoration of our whole spiritual life by intercourse with God. Learn to believe in God, to take hold of God, to let God take possession of your your life, and it will be easy to take hold of the promise. He who knows and trusts God finds it easy to trust the promise too.

Just note how distinctly this comes out in the saints of old. Every special exhibition of the power of faith was the fruit of a special revelation of God. See it in Abraham: "And *the word of the Lord came* unto Abram, saying, Fear not, Abram; *I am thy shield.* And *he brought him forth* abroad, *and said . . .* And he believed the Lord." And later: "The Lord *appeared unto him and said* unto him, I am God Almighty. And Abram fell on his face, and *God talked with him,* saying, As for me, behold my covenant is with thee." It was the revelation of God Himself that gave the promise its living power to enter the heart and work the faith. Because they knew God, these men of faith could not do anything but trust His promise. God's promise will be to us what God Himself is. It is the man who walks before the Lord, and falls on his face to listen while the living God speaks to him, who will really receive the promise. Though we have God's promises in the Bible, with full liberty to take them, the spiritual power is wanting, except as *God Himself speaks them to us. And He speaks to those who walk and live with Him.* Therefore, have faith in God: let faith be all eye and ear, the surrender to let God make His full impression, and reveal Himself fully in the soul. Count it one of the chief blessings of prayer to exercise faith in God, as the living mighty God who waits to fulfill in us all the good pleasure of His will, and the work of faith with power. See in Him the God of love, whose delight it is to bless and impart Himself. In such worship of faith in God the power will speedily come to believe the promise too: "All things whatsoever ye pray and ask for believe that ye receive." Yes, see that in faith you make God your own; the promise will be yours too.

Precious lesson that Jesus has to teach us this day. We seek God's gifts: God wants to give us Himself first. We think of prayer as the power to draw down good gifts from heaven; Jesus as the means to draw ourselves up to God. We want to stand at the door and cry; Jesus would have us first enter in and realize that we are friends and children. Let us accept the teaching. Let every experience of the littleness of our faith in prayer urge us first to have and exercise more faith in the living God, and in such faith to yield ourselves to Him. A heart full of God has power for the prayer of faith. Faith in God begets faith in the promise, in the promise too of an answer to prayer.

Therefore, child of God, take time, take time, to bow before *Him*, to wait on *Him* to reveal *Himself*. Take time, and let your soul in holy awe and worship exercise and express its faith in the Infinite One, and as He imparts Himself and takes possession of you, the prayer of faith will crown your faith in God.

*   *   *   *   *

O my God! I do believe in You. I believe in You as the Father, infinite in Your love and power. And as the Son, my Redeemer and my Life. And as the Holy Spirit, Comforter and Guide and Strength. Three-One God, I have faith in You. I know and am sure that all that You are You are to me, that all You have promised You will perform.

Lord Jesus, increase this faith. Teach me to take time, and wait and worship in the holy presence until my faith takes in all there is in my God for me. Let it see Him as the Fountain of all Life, working with almighty strength to accomplish His will on the world and in me. Let it see Him in His love longing to meet and fulfill my desires. Let it so take possession of my heart and life that through faith God alone may dwell there. Lord Jesus, help me! With my whole heart would I believe in God. Let faith in God each moment fill me.

O my Blessed Savior, how can Your church glorify You, how can it fulfill that work of intercession through which Your kingdom must come, unless our whole life be faith in God. Blessed Lord, speak Your word, "Have faith in God," into the depths of our souls. Amen.

13 The Cure for Little Faith

Then came the disciples to Jesus apart, and said, Why could not we cast him out? And he saith unto them, Because of your little faith: for verily I say unto you, If ye have faith as a grain of mustard seed . . . nothing shall be impossible unto you. Howbeit this kind goeth not out but by prayer and fasting.
Matthew 17:19-21

When the disciples saw Jesus cast the evil spirit out of the epileptic whom "they could not cure," they asked the Master for the cause of their failure. He had given them power and authority over all devils, and to cure all diseases. They had often exercised that power, and joyfully told how the devils were subject to them. And yet now, while He was on the Mount, they had utterly failed. That there had been nothing in the will of God or in the nature of the case to render deliverance impossible, had been proved: at Christ's bidding the evil spirit had gone out. From their expression, "Why could not we?" it is evident that they had wished and sought to do so; they had probably used the Master's name and called on the evil spirit to come out. Their efforts had been vain and, in presence of the multitude, they had been put to shame. "Why could not we?"

Christ's answer was direct and plain: it was because of your lack of faith. The cause of His success and their failure was not due to His having a special power to which they had no access. No; the reason was not hard to find. He had so often taught them that there is one power, that of faith, to which in the kingdom of darkness, as in the kingdom of God, everything must bow; in the spiritual world failure has but one cause, the lack of faith. Faith is the one condition on which all divine power can enter into man and work through him. It is the susceptibility of the unseen: man's will yielded up to, and molded by, the will of God. The power they had received to cast out devils, they did not hold in themselves as a permanent gift or possession; the power was in Christ, to be received, and held, and used by faith alone, living faith in Himself. Had they been full of faith *in Him* as Lord and Conqueror in the spirit world, had they been full of faith *in Him* as having given them authority to cast out in His name, this faith would have given them the victory. Their lack of faith was, for all time, the Master's explanation and reproof of impotence and failure in His church.

But such lack of faith must have a cause too. Well might the disciples have asked: "And why could we not believe? Our faith has cast out devils before this: why have we now failed in believing?" The Master proceeds to tell them before they ask: "This kind goeth not out but by fasting and prayer." As faith is the simplest, so it is the highest exercise of the spiritual life, where our spirit yields itself in perfect receptivity to God's Spirit, and so is strengthened to its highest activity. This faith depends entirely on the state of the spiritual life; only when this is strong and in full health, when the Spirit of God has full sway in our life, is there the power of faith to do its mighty deeds. And therefore Jesus adds: "Howbeit this kind goeth not out but by fasting and prayer." The faith that can overcome such stubborn resistance as you have just seen in this evil spirit, Jesus tells them, is not possible except to men living in very close fellowship with God, and in very special separation from the world—in prayer and fasting. So He teaches us two lessons in regard to prayer of deep importance. The one, that faith needs a life of prayer in which to grow and keep strong. The other, that prayer needs fasting for its full and perfect development.

Faith needs a life of prayer for its full growth. In all the different parts of the spiritual life there is such union, such unceasing action and reaction, that each may be both cause and effect. Thus it is with faith. There can be no true prayer without faith; some measure of faith must precede prayer. And yet prayer is also the way to more faith; there can be no higher degrees of faith except through much prayer. This is the lesson Jesus teaches here. There is nothing that needs to grow as much as our faith. "Your faith groweth exceedingly," is said of one church. When Jesus spoke the words, "According to your faith be it unto you," He announced the law of the kingdom, which tells us that all have not equal degrees of faith, that the same person has not always the same degree, and that the measure of faith must always determine the measure of power and of blessing. If we want to know where and how our faith is to grow, the Master points us to the throne of God. It is in prayer, in the exercise of the faith I have in fellowship with the living God, that faith can increase. Faith can live only by feeding on what is divine, on God Himself.

It is in the adoring worship of God, the waiting on Him and for Him, the deep silence of soul that yields itself for God to reveal Himself, that the capacity for knowing and trusting God will be developed. It is as we take His word from the blessed Book, and bring it to Himself, asking Him to speak that word to us with His living, loving voice, that the power will come fully to believe and receive the word as God's own word to us. It is in prayer, in living contact with God in living faith, that faith, the power to trust God, and in that trust, to accept everything He says, to accept every possibility He has offered to our faith, will become strong in us. Many Christians cannot understand what is meant by the much prayer they sometimes hear spoken of: they can form no conception, nor do they feel the need, of spending hours with God. But what the Master says, the experience of His people has confirmed: men of strong faith are men of much prayer.

This just brings us back again to the lesson we learned when Jesus, before telling us to believe that we receive what we ask, first said, "Have faith in God." It is God, the living God, into whom our faith must strike its roots deep and broad; then it will be strong to remove mountains and cast out devils. "If ye have faith . . . nothing shall be impossible to you."

If we would only give ourselves up to the work God has for us in the world, coming into contact with the mountains and the devils there are to be cast away and cast out, we should soon comprehend the need there is of much faith, and of much prayer, as the soil in which faith alone can be cultivated. Christ Jesus is our life, the life of our faith too. It is His life in us that makes us strong, and makes us able to believe. It is in the dying to self which much prayer implies, in closer union to Jesus, that the spirit of faith will come in power. *Faith needs prayer* for its full growth.

And *prayer needs fasting* for its full growth: this is the second lesson. Prayer is the one hand with which we grasp the invisible; fasting, the other, with which we let loose and cast away the visible. In nothing is man more closely connected with the world of sense than in his need of food, and his enjoyment of it. It was the fruit, good for food, with which man was tempted and fell in Paradise. It was with bread to be made of stones that Jesus, when hungry, was tempted in the wilderness, and in fasting that He triumphed. The body has been redeemed to be a temple of the Holy Spirit; it is in body as well as spirit, it is especially, Scripture says, in eating and drinking, that we are to glorify God. It is to be feared that there are many Christians to whom this eating to the glory of God has not yet become a spiritual reality. And the first thought suggested by Jesus' words in regard to fasting and prayer is that it is only in a life of moderation and temperance and self-denial that there will be the heart or the strength to pray much.

But then there is also its more literal meaning. Sorrow and anxiety cannot eat: joy celebrates its feasts with eating and drinking. There may come times of intense desire, when it is strongly felt how the body, with its appetites, lawful though they be, still hinder the spirit in its battle with the powers of darkness, and the need is felt of keeping it under. We are creatures of the senses: our mind is helped by what comes to us embodied in concrete form; fasting helps to express, to deepen, and to confirm the resolution that we are ready to sacrifice anything, to sacrifice ourselves, to attain what we seek for the kingdom of God. And He who accepted the fasting and sacrifice of the Son, knows how to value and accept and reward with spiritual power the soul that is ready to give up all for Christ and His kingdom.

And then follows a still wider application. Prayer is the reaching out after God and the unseen; fasting, the letting go of all that is of the seen and temporal. While ordinary Christians imagine that all that is not postively forbidden and sinful is lawful to them, and seek to retain as much as possible of this world, with its property, its literature, its enjoyments, the truly consecrated soul is as the soldier who carries only what he needs for the warfare. Laying aside every weight, as well as the easily besetting sin, afraid of entangling himself with the affairs of this life, he seeks to lead a Nazarite life, as one especially set apart for the Lord and His service. Without such voluntary separation, even from what is lawful, no one will attain power in prayer: this kind goes not out except by fasting and prayer.

Disciples of Jesus, who have asked the Master to teach you to pray, come now and accept His lessons. He tells you that prayer is the path to faith, strong faith, that can cast out devils. He tells you: "If ye have faith . . . nothing shall be impossible to you"; let this glorious promise encourage you to pray much. Is the prize not worth the price? Shall we not give up all to follow Jesus in the path He opens to us here; shall we not, if need be, fast? Shall we not do anything that neither the body nor the world around hinders us in our great life work—having intercourse with our God in prayer, that we may become men of faith, whom He can use in His work of saving the world.

* * * * *

Lord Jesus, how continually You have to reprove us for our unbelief! How strange it must appear to You, this terrible incapacity of trusting our Father and His promises. Lord, let Your reproof, with its searching "Because of your lack of faith," sink into the very depths of our hearts, and reveal to us how much of the sin and suffering around us is our own fault. And then teach us, blessed Lord, that there is a place where faith can be learned and gained—even in the prayer and fasting that brings us into living and abiding fellowship with Yourself and the Father.

O Savior, You are the Author and the Perfecter of our faith; teach us what it is to let You live in us by Your Holy Spirit. Lord, our efforts and prayers for grace to believe have been so unavailing. We know why it was: we sought for strength in ourselves to be given from You. Jesus, do at length teach us the mystery of Your life in us, and how You, by Your Spirit, undertakes to live in us the life of faith, to see to it that our faith shall not fail. Let us see that our faith will just be a part of that wonderful prayer life that You give in them who expect their training for the ministry of intercession, not in word and thought only, but in the holy unction You give, the inflowing of the Spirit of Your own life. And teach us how, in fasting and prayer, we may grow up to the faith to which nothing shall be impossible. Amen.

14 Prayer and Love

And whensoever ye stand praying, forgive, if ye have aught against any one; that your Father also who is in heaven may forgive you your trespasses.

Mark 11:25

These words follow immediately on the great prayer-promise, "All things whatsoever ye pray . . . believe that ye receive them, and ye shall have them." We have already seen how the words that preceded that promise, "have faith in God," taught us that in prayer all depends on our relation to God being clear; these words that follow on it remind us that our relation with fellowmen must be clear too. Love to God and love to our neighbor are inseparable: the prayer from a heart, that is either not right with God on the one hand, or with men on the other, cannot prevail. Faith and love are essential to each other.

We find that this is a thought to which our Lord frequently gave expression. In the Sermon on the Mount (Matt. 5:23, 24), when speaking of the sixth commandment, He taught His disciples how impossible acceptable worship to the Father was if everything was not right with a brother: "If therefore thou art offering thy gift at the altar, and there rememberest that thy brother hath aught against thee, leave there thy gift before the altar, and go thy way, first be reconciled to thy brother, and then come and offer thy gift." And so later, when speaking of prayer to God, after having taught us to pray, "Forgive us our debts, as we also have forgiven our debtors," He added at the close of the prayer: "If you forgive not men their trespasses, neither will your Father forgive your trespasses." At the close of the parable of the unmerciful servant He applies His teaching in the words: "So shall also my heavenly Father do unto you, if ye forgive not every one his brother from your hearts." And so here, beside the dried-up fig tree, where He speaks of the wonderful power of faith and the prayer of faith, He all at once, apparently without connection, introduces the thought, "Whensoever ye stand praying, forgive, if ye have aught against any one; that your Father also who is in heaven may forgive you your trespasses." It is as if the Lord had learned during His life at Nazareth and afterward that disobedience to the law of love to men was the great sin even of praying people, and the great cause of the feebleness of their prayer. And it is as if He wanted to lead us into His own blessed experience that nothing gives such liberty of access and such power in believing as the consciousness that we have given ourselves in love and compassion for those whom God loves.

The first lesson taught here is that of a forgiving disposition. We pray, "Forgive, *even as* we have forgiven." Scripture says, "Forgive one another, even as God also in Christ forgave you." God's full and free forgiveness is to be the rule of ours with men. Otherwise our reluctant, half-hearted forgiveness, which is not forgiveness at all, will be God's rule with us. Every prayer rests on our faith in God's pardoning grace. If God dealt with us after our sins, not one prayer could be heard. Pardon opens the door to all God's love and blessing: because God has pardoned all our sin, our prayer can prevail to obtain all we need. The deep sure ground of answer to prayer is God's forgiving love. When it has taken possession of the heart, we pray in faith. But also, when it has taken possession of the heart, we live in love. God's forgiving disposition, revealed in His love to us, becomes a disposition in us; as the power of His forgiving love shed abroad and dwelling within us, we forgive even as He forgives. If there is great and grievous injury or injustice done us, we seek first of all to possess a godlike disposition; to be kept from a sense of wounded honor, from a desire to maintain our rights, or from rewarding the offender as he has deserved. In the little annoyances of daily life we are watchful not to excuse the hasty temper, the sharp word, the quick judgment, with the thought that we mean no harm, that we do not keep the anger long, or that it would be too much to expect from feeble human nature that we should really forgive the way God and Christ do. No, we take the command literally, "*Even as* Christ forgave, *so also* do ye." The blood that cleanses the conscience from dead works, cleanses from selfishness too; the love it reveals is pardoning love, which takes possession of us and flows through us to others. Our forgiving love to others is the evidence of the reality of God's forgiving love in us, and so the condition of the prayer of faith.

There is a second, more general lesson: our daily life in the world is made the rest of our intercourse with God in prayer. How often the Christian, when he comes to pray, does his utmost to cultivate certain frames of mind that he thinks will be pleasing. He does not understand, or forgets, that life does not consist of so many loose pieces, of which now the one, then the other, can be taken up. Life is a whole, and the pious frame of the hour of prayer is judged by God from the ordinary frame of the daily life of which the hour of prayer is but a small part. Not the feeling I call up, but the tone of my life during the day, is God's criterion of what I really am and desire. My drawing near to God is of one piece with my intercourse with men and earth: failure here will cause failure there. And that not only when there is the distinct consciousness of anything wrong between my neighbor and myself, but the ordinary current of my thinking and judging, the unloving thoughts and words I allow to pass unnoticed, can hinder my prayer. The effectual prayer of faith comes out from a life given up to the will and the love of God. Not according to what I try to be when praying, but when I am not praying, is my prayer dealt with by God.

We may gather these thoughts into a third lesson: in our life with others the one thing on which everything depends is love. The spirit of forgiveness is the spirit of love. Because God is love, He forgives: it is only when we are dwelling in love that we can forgive as God forgives. In love to the brethren we have the evidence of love to the Father, the ground of confidence before God, and the assurance that our prayer will be heard (1 John 4:20; 3:18-21, 23). "Let us love . . . in deed and truth. *Hereby* shall we . . . assure our heart before Him. . . . If our heart condemn us not, we have boldness toward God; and whatsoever we ask we receive of him." Neither faith nor work will profit if we do not have love; it is love that unites with God, it is love that proves the reality of faith. As essential as in the word that precedes the great prayer-promise in Mark 11:24, "Have faith in God," is this one that follows it, "Have love to men." The right relations to the living God above me, and the living men around me, are the conditions of effectual prayer.

This love is of special consequence when we labor and pray for them. We sometimes give ourselves to work for Christ, from zeal for His cause, as we call it, or for our own spiritual health, without giving ourselves in personal self-sacrificing love for those whose souls we seek. No wonder that our faith is feeble and does not conquer. To look on each wretched one, however unlovable he is, in the light of the tender love of Jesus the Shepherd seeking the lost; to see Jesus Christ in him, and to take him up, for Jesus' sake, in a heart that really loves—this is the secret of believing prayer and successful effort. Jesus, in speaking of forgiveness, speaks of love as its root. Just as in the Sermon on the Mount He connected His teaching and promises about prayer with the call to be merciful, as the Father in heaven is merciful (Matt. 5:7, 8, 22, 38-48), so we see it here: a loving life is the condition of believing prayer.

It has been said that there is nothing so heart-searching as believing prayer, or even the honest effort to pray in faith. Let us not turn the edge of that self-examination by the thought that God does not hear our prayer for reasons known to Himself alone. By no means, "Ye ask and receive not, because ye ask amiss." Let that word of God search us. Let us ask whether our prayer is indeed the expression of a life wholly given over to the will of God and the love of man. Love is the only soil in which faith can strike its roots and thrive. As it throws its arms up, and opens it heart heavenward, the Father always looks to see if it has them opened toward the evil and the unworthy too. In that love, not indeed the love of perfect attainment, but the love of fixed purpose and sincere obedience, faith can alone obtain the blessing. The person who gives himself to let the love of God dwell in him, and in the practice of daily life to love as God loves, will have the power to believe in the love that hears his every prayer. It is *the Lamb,* who is in the midst of the throne: it is suffering and forbearing love that prevails with God in prayer. The merciful shall obtain mercy; the meek shall inherit the earth.

* * * * *

Blessed Father, You are love, and only he who abides in love abides in You and in fellowship with You. The blessed Son has this day again taught me how deeply true this is of my fellowship with You in prayer. O my God, let Your love, shed abroad in my heart by the Holy Spirit, be in me a fountain of love to all around me, that out of a life in love may spring the power of believing prayer. Father, grant by the Holy Spirit that this may be my experience, that a life in love to all around me is the gate to a life in the love of my God. And give me especially to find in the joy with which I forgive day by day whoever might offend me, the proof that Your forgiveness to me is a power and a life.

Lord Jesus, my blessed Teacher, teach me to forgive and to love. Let the power of Your blood make the pardon of my sins such a reality, that forgiveness, as shown by You to me, and by me to others, may be the very joy of heaven. Show me whatever in my intercourse with fellow men might hinder my fellowship with God, so that my daily life in my own home and in society may be the school in which strength and confidence are gathered for the prayer of faith. Amen.

15 *The Power of United Prayer*

Again I say unto you, that if two of you shall agree on earth as touching anything that they shall ask, it shall be done for them of my Father who is in heaven. For where two or three are gathered together in my name, there am I in the midst of them.

Matthew 18:19, 20

One of the first lessons of our Lord in His school of prayer was: not to be seen of men. Enter your inner chamber; be alone with the Father. When He has taught us that the meaning of prayer is personal individual contact with God, He comes with a second lesson: you have need not only of secret solitary, but also of public united prayer. And He gives us a special promise for the united prayer of two or three who agree in what they ask. As a tree has its root hidden in the ground and its stem growing up into the sunlight, so prayer needs equally for its full development the hidden secrecy in which the soul meets God alone, and the public fellowship with those who find in the name of Jesus their common meeting place.

The reason why this must be so is plain. The bond that unites a man to his fellowmen is no less real and close than that which unites him to God: he is one with them. Grace renews not alone our relation to God but to man too. We learn not only to say "My Father," but "Our Father." Nothing would be more unnatural than that the children of a family should always meet their father separately, but never in the united expression of their desires or their love. Believers are not only members of one family, but also of one body. Just as each member of the body depends on the other, and the full action of the spirit dwelling in the body depends on the union and cooperation of all, so Christians cannot reach the full blessing God is ready to bestow through His Spirit, but as they seek and receive it in fellowship with each other. It is in the union and fellowship of believers that the Spirit can manifest its full power. It was to the 120 continuing in one place together, and praying with one accord, that the Spirit came from the throne of the glorified Lord.

The marks of true united prayer are given us in these words of our Lord. The first is *agreement* as to the thing asked. There must not only be generally the consent to agree with anything another may ask: there must be some special matter of distinct, united desire; the agreement must be, as all prayer, in spirit and in truth. In such agreement it will become clear to us what exactly we are asking, whether we may confidently ask according to God's will, and whether we are ready to believe that we have received what we ask.

The second mark is the gathering in, or into, the name of Jesus. We shall later have much more to learn of the need and the power of the name of Jesus in prayer; here our Lord teaches us that the name must be the center of union to which believers gather, the bond of union that makes them one, just as a home contains and unites all who are in it. "The name of the Lord is a strong tower; the righteous runneth into it and escape." That name is such a reality to those who understand and believe it that to meet within it is to have Himself present. The love and unity of His disciples have to Jesus infinite attraction: "Where two or three are gathered in my name, *there am I in the midst of them.*" It is the living presence of Jesus, in the fellowship of His loving, praying disciples, that gives united prayer its power.

The third mark is the sure answer: "It shall be done for them of my Father." A prayer meeting for maintaining religious fellowship, or seeking our own edification, may have its use; this was not the Savior's view in its appointment. He meant it as a means of securing *special answer to prayer.* A prayer meeting without recognized answer to prayer ought to be an anomaly. When anyone of us has distinct desires in regard to which we feel too weak to exercise the needful faith, we ought to seek strength in the help of others. In the unity of faith and of love and of the Spirit, the power of the name and the presence of Jesus acts more freely and the answer comes more surely. The mark that there has been true united prayer is the fruit, the answer, the receiving of the thing we have asked: "I say unto you, *it shall be done* for them of my Father who is in heaven."

What an unspeakable privilege united prayer is, and what a power it might be. If the believing husband and wife knew that they were joined together in the name of Jesus to experience His presence and power in united prayer (1 Peter); if friends believed what mighty help two or three praying in concert could give each other; if in every prayer meeting the coming together in the name, the faith in the presence, and the expectation of the answer, stood in the foreground; if in every church united effectual prayer were regarded as one of the chief purposes for which they are banded together, the highest exercise of their power as a church; if in the church universal the coming of the kingdom, the coming of the King Himself, first in the mighty outpouring of His Holy Spirit, then in His own glorious person, were really a matter of unceasing united crying to God—who can say what blessing might come to and through those who thus agreed to prove God in the fulfillment of His promise.

In the Apostle Paul we see distinctly what a reality his faith in the power of united prayer was. To the Romans he writes (15:30): "I beseech you, brethren . . . by the love of the Spirit, that ye *strive together with me* in your prayers to God for me." He expects in answer to be delivered from his enemies, and to be prospered in his work. To the Corinthians (2 Cor. 1:10-11), "[God] will still deliver us, ye also helping together on our behalf by your supplication;" their prayer is to have a real share in his deliverance. To the Ephesians he writes: "With all prayer and supplication praying at all seasons in the Spirit . . . for all the saints . . . and on my behalf, that utterance may be given unto me." (6:18, 20). His power and success in his ministry he makes to depend on their prayers. With the Philippians (1:19) he expects that his trials will turn to his salvation and the progress of the gospel "*through your supplication and* the supply of the Spirit of Jesus Christ." To the Colossians (4:3) he adds to the injunction to continue steadfast in prayer: "Withal praying for us also; that God may open unto us a door for the word." And to the Thessalonians (2 Thess. 3:1) he writes: "Finally, brethren, pray for us, that the word of the Lord may run and be glorified . . . and that we may be delivered from unreasonable and evil men." It is everywhere evident that Paul felt himself the member of a body, on the sympathy and cooperation of which he was dependent and that he counted on the prayers of the churches to gain for him, what otherwise might not be given. The prayers of the church were to him as real a factor in the work of the kingdom as the power of God.

Who can say what power a church could develop and exercise, if it gave itself to the work of prayer day and night for the coming of the kingdom, for God's power on His servants and His word, for the glorifying of God in the salvation of souls? Most churches think their members are gathered into one simply to take care of and build up each other. They do not know that God rules the world by the prayers of His saints; that prayer is the power by which Satan is conquered; that by prayer the church on earth has disposal of the powers of the heavenly world. They do not remember that Jesus has, by His promise, consecrated every assembly in His name to be a gate of heaven, where His presence is to be felt, and His power experienced in the Father fulfilling their desires.

We cannot sufficiently thank God for the blessed week of united prayer, which in many churches opens every year. As proof of our unity and our faith in the power of united prayer, as a training school for the enlargement of our hearts to take in all the needs of the church universal, as a help to united persevering prayer, it is of unspeakable value. But it is especially valuable as a stimulus to continued union in prayer in the smaller circles. And it will become even greater, as God's people recognize what it is, all to meet as one in the name of Jesus, to have His presence in the midst of a body all united in the Holy Spirit, and boldly to claim the promise that it shall be done of the Father what they agree to ask.

Blessed Lord who in Your high-priestly prayer ask so earnestly for the unity of Your people, teach us how You invite and urge us to this unity by Your precious promise given to united prayer. It is when we are one in love and desire that our faith has Your presence and the Father's answer.

Father, we pray for Your people, and for every smaller circle of those who meet together, that they may be one. Remove, we pray, all selfishness and self-interest, all narrowness of heart and estrangement by which that unity is hindered. Cast out the spirit of the world and the flesh, through which Your promise loses all its power. O let the thought of Your presence and the Father's favor draw us all nearer to each other.

Grant especially, blessed Lord, that Your church may believe that it is by the power of united prayer that she can bind and loose in heaven; that Satan can be cast out; that souls can be saved; that mountains can be removed; that the kingdom can be hastened. And grant, good Lord, that in the circle with which I pray, the prayer of the church may indeed be the power through which Your name and Word are glorified. Amen.

16 The Power of Persevering Prayer

And he spake a parable unto them to the end that they ought always to pray, and not to faint. . . . And the Lord said, Hear what the unrighteous judge saith. And shall not God avenge his elect, that cry to him day and night, and yet he is longsuffering over them? I say unto you, that he will avenge them speedily.

Luke 18:1-8

Of all the mysteries of the prayer world, the need for persevering prayer is one of the greatest. That the Lord, who is so loving and longing to bless, should have to be supplicated time after time, sometimes year after year, before the answer comes, we cannot easily understand. It is also one of the greatest practical difficulties in the exercise of believing prayer. When, after persevering supplication, our prayer remains unanswered, it is often easiest for our slothful flesh, and it has all the appearance of pious submission, to think that we must now cease praying, because God may have His secret reason for withholding His answer to our request.

It is by faith alone that the difficulty is overcome. When once faith has taken its stand on God's word, and the name of Jesus, and has yielded itself to the leading of the Spirit to seek God's will and honor alone in its prayer, it need not be discouraged by delay. It knows from Scripture that the power of believing prayer is simply irresistible; real faith can never be disappointed. It knows how, to exercise the irresistible power it can have. Just as water must be gathered up and accumulated until the stream can come down in full force, so must there often be a heaping up of prayer until God sees that the measure is full, and the answer comes. It knows that just as the farmer has to take his ten thousand steps and sow his ten thousand seeds, and each one a part of the preparation for the final harvest, so there is a need for oft-repeated persevering prayer, all working out some desired blessing. It knows for certain that not a single believing prayer can fail of its effect in heaven, but has its influence, and is treasured up to work out an answer in due time to him who perseveres to the end. It knows that it has to do not with human thoughts or possibilities, but with the word of the living God. And so, even as Abraham through so many years "in hope believed against hope," and then "through faith *and patience* inherited the promise," it is a fact that the longsuffering of the Lord is salvation, *waiting* and *hastening* to the coming of its Lord to fulfill His promise.

To enable us, when the answer to our prayer does not come at once, to combine quiet patience and joyful confidence in our persevering prayer, we must especially try to understand the two words in which our Lord sets forth the character and conduct, not of the unjust judge, but of our God and Father, toward those whom He allows to cry day and night to Him: "He is *longsuffering* over them . . . he will avenge them *speedily*."

He will avenge them *speedily*, the Master says. The blessing is all prepared; He is not only willing but most anxious to give them what they ask; everlasting love burns with the longing desire to reveal itself fully to its beloved, and to satisfy their needs. God will not delay one moment longer than is absolutely necessary; He will do all in His power to hasten and speed the answer.

But why, if this is true and His power is definite, does it often take so long for an answer to prayer? And why must God's own elect so often, in the midst of suffering and conflict, cry day and night? "He is *longsuffering* over them." "Behold! the husbandman waiteth for the precious fruit of the earth, being [*long-suffering*] over it, until it receive the early and the latter rain." The husbandman does indeed long for his harvest, but knows that it must have its full time of sunshine and rain, and has long patience. A child so often wants to pick the half-ripe fruit; the husbandman knows to wait until the proper time. Man, in his spiritual nature too, is under the law of gradual growth that reigns in all created life. It is only in the path of development that he can reach his divine destiny. And it is the Father, in whose hands are the times and seasons, who alone knows the moment when the soul or the church is ripened to that fullness of faith in which it can really take and keep the blessing. As a father who longs to have his only child home from school, and yet waits patiently until the time at school is completed, so it is with God and His children: He is the longsuffering One, and answers speedily.

The insight into this truth leads the believer to cultivate the corresponding dispositions: *patience* and *faith, waiting* and *hasting,* are the secret of his perseverance. By faith in the promise of God, we know that we *have* the petitions we have asked of Him. Faith takes and holds the answer in the promise, as an unseen spiritual possession, rejoices in it, and praises for it. But there is a difference between the faith that thus holds the word and knows that it has the answer, and the clearer, fuller, riper faith that obtains the promise as a present experience. It is in persevering, not unbelieving, but confident and praising prayer, that the soul grows up into that full union with its Lord in which it can enter upon the possession of the blessing in Him. There may be in some things about us, there may be in that great system of being of which we are part, there may be in God's government, things that have to be put right through our prayer, before the answer can fully come: the faith that has, according to the command, believed that it has received, can allow God to take His time; it knows it has prevailed and must prevail. In quiet, persistent, and determined perseverance it continues in prayer and thanksgiving until the blessing comes. So we see combined what at first appears so contradictory; the faith that rejoices in the answer of the unseen God as a present possession, with the patience that cries day and night until it be revealed. The *speedily* of God's *longsuffering* is met by the triumphant but patient faith of His waiting child.

Our great danger in this school of the answer delayed, is

the temptation of thinking that, after all, it may not be God's will to give us what we ask. If our prayer is according to God's word, and under the leading of the Spirit, let us not give way to these fears. Let us learn to give God time. God needs time with us. If we only give Him time, that is, time in the daily fellowship with Himself, for Him to exercise the full influence of His presence on us, and time, day by day, in the course of our being kept waiting, for faith to prove its reality and to fill our whole being, He Himself will lead us from faith to vision; we shall see the glory of God. Let no delay shake our faith. Of faith it holds good: first the blade, then the ear, then the full corn in the ear. Each believing prayer beings us a step nearer the final victory. Each believing prayer helps to ripen the fruit and bring us nearer to it; it fills up the measure of prayer and faith known to God alone; it conquers the hindrances in the unseen world; it hastens the end. Child of God, give the Father time. He is longsuffering with you. He wants the blessing to be rich, and full, and sure; give Him time, while you cry day and night. Only remember the word: "I say unto you . . . he will avenge them speedily."

The blessing of such persevering prayer is unspeakable. There is nothing so heart-searching as the prayer of faith. It teaches you to discover and confess, and give up everything that hinders the coming of the blessing; everything you have may be not in accordance with the Father's will. It leads to closer fellowship with Him who alone can teach to pray, to a more entire surrender to draw nigh under no covering but that of the blood, and the Spirit. It calls to a closer and more simple abiding in Christ alone. Give God time. He will perfect that which concerns you. "Longsuffering—speedily," this is God's watchword as you enter the gates of prayer: let it be yours too.

Let it be so for you whether you pray for yourself, or for others. All labor, bodily and mental, needs time and effort: we must give up *ourselves* to it. Nature discovers her secrets and yields her treasures only to diligent and thoughtful labor. However little we can understand it, in the spiritual harvest it is the same: the seed we sow in the soil of heaven, the efforts we put forth, and the influence we seek to exert in the world above, need our whole being: we must *give ourselves* to prayer. But let us hold fast to the great confidence, that in due season we shall reap, if we do not faint or become weary.

And let us especially learn the lesson as we pray for the church of Christ. She is indeed as the poor widow, in the absence of her Lord, apparently at the mercy of her adversary, helpless to obtain redress. Let us, when we pray for His church or any portion of it, that is under the power of the world, ask Him to visit her with the mighty workings of His Spirit and to prepare her for His coming. Let us pray in the assured faith that prayer does help, that praying always and not fainting will bring the answer. Only give God time. And then keep crying day and night. "Hear what the righteous judge saith. And shall not God avenge his elect, that cry to him day and night, and yet *he is longsuffering* over them? I say unto you, that *he will avenge them speedily.*"

* * * * *

O Lord my God, teach me now to know Your way, and in faith to apprehend what Your beloved Son has taught: "he will avenge them speedily." Let Your tender love, and the delight You have in hearing and blessing Your children, lead me implicitly to accept Your promise, that we receive what we believe, that we have the petitions we ask, and that the answer will in due time be seen. Lord, we understand the seasons in nature, and know to wait with patience for the fruit we long for—O fill us with the assurance that not one moment longer than is needed wilt You delay, and that faith will hasten the answer.

Blessed Master, You have said that it is a sign of God's elect that they cry day and night. O teach us to understand this. You knowest how soon we grow faint and weary. It is as if the divine majesty is so much beyond the need or the reach of continued supplication, that it does not become us to be too importunate. O Lord, teach me how real the labor of prayer is. I know how here on earth, when I have failed in an undertaking, I can often succeed by renewed and more continuing effort, by giving more time and thought: show me how, by giving myself more entirely to prayer, to live in prayer, I shall obtain what I ask. And above all, O my blessed Teacher! Author and Perfector of faith, let by Your grace my whole life be one of faith in the Son of God who loved me and gave Himself for me—in whom my prayer gains acceptance, in whom I have the assurance of the answer, in whom the answer will be mine. Lord Jesus, in this faith I will pray always and not faint. Amen.

17 Prayer in Harmony With the Being of God

Father, I thank thee that thou heardest me. And I knew that thou hearest me always.

John 11:41, 42

Thou art my Son; this day have I begotten thee. Ask of me, and I will give thee.

Psalm 2:7, 8

In the New Testament we find a distinction made between faith and knowledge. "To one is given through the Spirit the word of *wisdom*; and to another the word of *knowledge*, according to the same Spirit: to another *faith*, in the same Spirit." In a child or in an immature Christian there may be much faith with little knowledge. Childlike simplicity accepts the truth without difficulty, and often cares little to give itself or others any reason for its faith but this: God has said. But it is the will of God that we should love and serve Him, not only with all the heart but also with all the mind; that we should grow up into an insight into the divine wisdom and beauty of all His ways and words and works. It is only in this way that the believer will be fully able to approach and rightly to adore the glory of God's grace; and only in this way that our heart can intelligently apprehend the treasures of wisdom and knowledge there are in redemption, and be prepared to enter fully into the highest note of the song that rises before the throne: "O the depth of the riches both of the wisdom and the knowledge of God!"

In our prayer life this truth has its full application. While prayer and faith are so simple that the new-born convert can pray with power, true Christian science finds in the doctrine of prayer some of its deepest problems. In how far is the power of prayer a reality? And, how can God grant to prayer such mighty power? How can the action of prayer be harmonized with the will and the decrees of God? How can God's sovereignty and our will, God's liberty and ours, be reconciled? These and other like questions are fit subjects for Christian meditation and inquiry. The more earnestly and reverently we approach such mysteries, the more we shall in adoring wonder fall down to praise Him who has in prayer given such power to man.

One of the secret difficulties with regard to prayer—one which, though not expressed, does often really hinder prayer—is derived from the perfection of God, in His absolute independence of all that is outside of Himself. Is He not the Infinite Being, who owes what He is to Himself alone, who determines Himself, and whose wise and holy will has determined all that is to be? How can prayer influence Him, or how can He be moved by prayer to do what otherwise would not be done? Is not the promise of an answer to prayer simply a condescension to our weakness? Is what is said of the power—the much-availing power—of prayer anything more than an accommodation to our mode of thought, because the Deity never can be dependent on an action from without for its doings? And is not the blessing of prayer simply the influence it exercises on ourselves?

In seeking an answer to such questions, we find the key in the very being of God, in the mystery of the Holy Trinity. If God was only one person, shut up within Himself, there could be no thought of nearness to Him or influence on Him. But in God there are three persons. In God we have Father and Son, who have in the Holy Spirit their living bond of unity and fellowship. When eternal love begat the Son, and the Father gave the Son as the second person a place next to Himself as His equal and His counselor, a way was opened for prayer and its influence in the inmost life of Deity itself. Just as on earth, so in heaven the whole relation between Father and Son is that of giving and taking. And if that taking is to be as voluntary and self-determined as the giving, there must be on the part of the Son an asking and receiving. In the holy fellowship of the divine persons, this asking of the Son was one of the great operations of the thrice blessed Life of God. Therefore we have it in Psalm 2: "This day I have begotten thee. Ask of me, and I will give thee." The Father gave the Son the place and the power to act upon Him. The asking of the Son was no mere show or shadow, but one of those life movements in which the love of the Father and the Son met and completed each other. The Father had determined that He should not be alone in His counsels: there was a Son on whose asking and accepting their fulfillment should depend. So there was in the very Being and Life of God an asking of which prayer on earth was to be the reflection and the outflow. It was not without including this that Jesus said, "I knew that thou hearest me always." Just as the sonship of Jesus on earth may not be separated from His sonship in heaven, even so with His prayer on earth, it is the continuation and the counterpart of His asking in heaven. The prayer of the man Christ Jesus is the link between the eternal asking of the only-begotten Son in the bosom of the Father and the prayer of men upon earth. Prayer has its rise and its deepest source in the very being of God. In the bosom of Deity nothing is ever done without prayer—the asking of the Son and the giving of the Father.

This may help us to somewhat understand how the prayer of man, coming through the Son, can have effect on God. The decrees of God are not decisions made by Him without reference to the Son, or His petition, or the petition to be sent up through Him. By no means. The Lord Jesus is the first-begotten, the Head and Heir of all things: all things were created *through Him* and *unto Him*, and all things consist *in Him*. In the counsels of the Father, the Son, as representative of all creation, always had a voice; in the decrees of the eternal purpose room was always left for the liberty of the Son as mediator and intercessor, and so for the petitions of all who draw near to the Father in the Son.

And if you think that this liberty and power of the Son to act upon the Father is at variance with the immutability of the divine decrees, let us not forget that there is not with God as with man, a past by which He is irrevocably bound. God does not live in time with its past and future; the distinctions of time have no reference to Him who inhabits eternity. And eternity is an ever-present now, in which the past is never past, and the future always present. To meet our human weakness, Scripture must speak of past decrees, and a coming future. In reality, the immutability of God's counsel is always in perfect harmony with His liberty to do whatever He wills. The Father-heart holds itself open and free to listen to every prayer that rises through the Son, and God indeed allows Himself to be moved by prayer to do what He otherwise would not have done.

This perfect harmony and union of divine sovereignty and human liberty is to us an unfathomable mystery, because God as "the Eternal One" transcends all our thoughts. But let it be our comfort and strength to be assured that the power of prayer has its origin and certainty in the eternal fellowship of the Father and the Son, and that through our union with the Son, our prayer is taken up and can have its influence in the inner life of the blessed Trinity. God's decrees are no iron framework against which man's liberty would vainly seek to struggle. No. God Himself is the living love, who in His Son as man has entered into the tenderest relation with all that is human, who through the Holy Spirit takes up all that is human into the Divine life of love, and keeps Himself free to give every human prayer its place in His government of the world.

It is in the daybreak light of such thoughts that the doctrine of the blessed Trinity no longer is an abstract speculation, but the living manifestation of the way in which it were possible for man to be taken up into the fellowship of God, and his prayer to become a real factor in God's rule of this earth. And we can, as in the distance, catch glimpses of the light that from the eternal world shines out on words such as these: 'Through him we have access by one Spirit unto the Father.'

* * * * *

Everlasting God, in deep reverence would I with veiled face worship before the holy mystery of Your divine being. And if it please You, O most glorious God, to unveil anything of that mystery, I would bow with fear and trembling, lest I sin against You, as I meditate on Your glory.

Father, I thank You that You bear this name not only as the Father of Your children here on earth, but as having from eternity subsisted as the Father with Your only-begotten Son. I thank You that as Father You can hear our prayer because You have from eternity given a place in Your counsels to the asking of Your Son. I thank You that we have seen in Him on earth, what blessed intercourse He had with You in heaven; and how from eternity in all Your counsels and decrees had room been left for His prayers and their answers. And I thank You above all that through His true human nature on Your throne above, and through Your Holy Spirit in our human nature here below, a way has been opened up by which every human cry of need can be taken up into and touch the life and the love of God, and receive in answer whatever it shall ask.

Blessed Jesus, in whom as the Son the path of prayer has been opened up, and who gives us assurances of the answer, we beseech You, teach Your people to pray. Ot let each day be the sign of our sonship, that, like You, we know that the Father hears us always. Amen.

18 Prayer in Harmony With the Destiny of Man

He saith unto them, Whose is this image and superscription?
Matthew 22:20

And God said, Let us make man in our image, after our likeness.

Genesis 1:26

Whose is this image? It was by this question that Jesus foiled His enemies when they thought to take Him, and settled the matter of duty in regard to the tribute. The question and the principle it involves are of universal application, nowhere more truly than in man himself. The image he bears decides his destiny. Bearing God's image, he belongs to God: prayer to God is what he was created for. Prayer is part of the wondrous likeness he bears to His divine original; of the deep mystery of the fellowship of love in which the Three-One has His blessedness, prayer is the earthly image and likeness.

The more we meditate on what prayer is, and the wonderful power with God that it has, the more we feel constrained to ask who and what man is, that such a place in God's counsels should have been alotted to him. Sin has so degraded him, that from what he is now, we can form no conception of what he was meant to be. We must turn back to God's own record of man's creation to discover there what God's purpose was, and with what capacities man was endowed for the fulfillment of that purpose.

Man's destiny appears clearly from God's language at creation. It was to *fill*, to *subdue*, to *have domination* over the earth and all in it. The three expressions show us that man was meant, as God's representative, to hold rule here on earth.

As God's viceroy he was to fill God's place: subject to God, he was to keep all else in subjection to Him. It was the will of God that all that was to be done on earth should be done through him: the history of the earth was to be entirely in his hands.

In accordance with such a destiny was the position he was to occupy, and the power at his disposal. When an earthly sovereign sends an ambassador to a distant country, it is understood that he advises as to the policy to be adopted, and that that advice is acted on. If his policy is not approved, he is recalled to make way for some one who better understands the country's situation; as long as he is trusted, his advice is carried out. As God's representative man was to have ruled; all was to have been done under his will and rule; on his advice and at his request heaven was to have bestowed its blessing on earth. His prayer was to have been the wonderful, though simple and most natural channel, in which the intercourse between the King in heaven and His faithful servant man, as lord of this world, was to have been maintained. The destinies of the world were given into the power of the wishes, the will, the prayer of man.

With sin all this underwent a terrible change: man's fall brought all creation under the curse. With redemption the beginning of a glorious restoration was seen. No sooner had God begun in Abraham to form for Himself a people from whom kings, yea, the great King, should come forth, than we see what power the prayer of God's faithful servant has to decide the destinies of those who come into contact with him. In Abraham we see how prayer is not only, or even chiefly, the means of obtaining blessing for ourselves, but is the exercise of his royal prerogative to influence the destinies of men, and the will of God that rules them. We do not once find Abraham praying for himself. His prayer for Sodom and Lot, for Abimelech, for Ishmael, prove what power a man, who is God's friend, has to make the history of those around him.

This had been man's destiny from the first. Scripture not only tells us this, but also teaches us how it was that God could entrust man with such a high calling. It was because He had created him *in His own image and likeness*. The external rule was not committed to him without the inner fitness: the bearing of God's image in having dominion, in being lord of all, had its root in the inner likeness, in his nature. There was an inner agreement and harmony between God and man, an incipient godlikeness, which gave man a real fitness for being the mediator between God and His world, for he was to be a prophet, priest, and king, to interpret God's will, to represent nature's needs, to receive and dispense God's bounty. It was in bearing God's image that he could bear God's rule; he was indeed so like God, so capable of entering into God's purposes, and carrying out His plans, that God could trust him with the wonderful privilege of asking and obtaining what the world might need. Although sin has for a time frustrated God's plans, prayer still remains what it would have been if man had never fallen: the proof of man's godlikeness, the vehicle of his intercourse with the infinite Unseen One, the power that is allowed to hold the hand that holds the destinies of the universe. Prayer is not merely the cry of the suppliant for mercy; it is the highest putting forth of his will by man, knowing himself to be of divine origin, created for and capable of being, in kinglike liberty, the executor of the the the counsels of the Eternal.

What sin destroyed, grace has restored. What the first Adam lost, the second has won back. In Christ man regains his original position, and the church, abiding in Christ, inherits the promise: "Ask what ye will, and it shall be done unto you." Such a promise does by no means, in the first place, refer to the grace or blessing we need for ourselves. It has reference to our position as the fruit-bearing branches of the heavenly Vine, who, like Him, only live for the work and glory of the Father. It is for those who abide in Him, who have forsaken self to take up their abode in Him with His life of obedience and self-sacrifice, who have lost their life and found it in Him, who are now entirely given up to the interests of the Father and His kingdom. These are they who understand how their new creation has brought them back to their original destiny, has restored God's image and likeness, and with it the power to have dominion. Such have indeed the power, each in their own circle, to obtain and dispense the powers of heaven here on earth. With holy boldness they may make known what they will: they live as priests in God's presence; as kings, the powers of the world to come begin to be at their disposal. They enter upon the fulfillment of the promise: "Ask whatsoever ye will, it shall be done unto you."

Church of the living God! your calling is higher and holier than you know. Through your members, as kings and priests to God, would God rule the world; their prayers bestow and withhold the blessings of heaven. In His elect who are not just content to be saved themselves, but yield themselves wholly, that through them, even as through the Son, the Father may fulfill all His glorious counsel, in these His elect, who cry day and night unto Him, God would prove how wonderdul man's original destiny was. As the image-bearer of God on earth, he found the earth given into his hand. When he fell, all fell with him: the whole creation groans and travails in pain together. But now he is redeemed; the restoration of the original dignity has begun. It is surely God's purpose that the fulfillment of His enternal purpose, and the coming of His kingdom, should depend on those of His people who, abiding in Christ, are ready to take up their position in Him their Head, the great Priest-King, and in their prayers are bold enough to say what they will that their God should do. As image-bearer and representative of God on earth, redeemed man has by his prayers to determine the history of this earth. Man was created, and has now again been redeemed, to pray, and by his prayer to have dominion.

* * * * *

Lord, what is man, that You are mindful of him? And the son of man, that You visit him? for You have made him a little lower than the angels, and have crowned him with glory and honor. You made him to have dominion over the work of Your hands: You have put all things under his feet. O Lord, our Lord, how excellent is Your name in all the earth!

Lord God, how low has sin made man to sink. And how terribly has it darkened his mind, that he does not even know his divine destiny, to be Your servant and representative. Alas! that even Your people, when their eyes are opened, are so unready to accept their calling and to seek to have power with God, that they may have power with men too to bless them.

Lord Jesus, it is in You the Father has again crowned man with glory and honor, and opened the way for us to be what He would have us. O Lord, have mercy on Your people, and visit Your heritage! Work mightily in Your church, and teach Your believing disciples to go forth in their royal priesthood and in the power of prayer, to which You have given such wonderful promises, to serve Your kingdom, to have rule over the nations, and make the name of God glorious in the earth. Amen.

19   *Power for Praying and Working*

Verily, verily, I say unto you, He that believeth on me, the works that I do shall he do also; and greater works than these shall he do; because I go unto the Father. And whatsoever ye shall ask in my name, that will I do.

John 14:12, 13

As the Savior opened His public ministry with His disciples by the Sermon on the Mount, so He closes it by the parting address preserved to us by John. In both He speaks more than once of prayer. But with a difference. In the Sermon on the Mount it is as to disciples who have only just entered His school, who scarcely know that God is their Father, and whose prayer chiefly has reference to their personal needs. In His closing address He speaks to disciples whose training time is now come to an end, and who are ready as His messengers to take His place and His work. In the former the chief lesson is: Be childlike, pray believingly, and trust the Father that He will give you all good gifts. Here He points to something higher: they are now His friends to whom He has made known all that He has heard of the Father; His messengers, who have entered His plans, and into whose hands the care of His work and kingdom on earth is to be entrusted. They are now to go out and do His works, and, in the power of His approaching exaltation, even greater works: prayer is now to be the channel through which that power is to be received for their work. With Christ's ascension to the Father a new era begins for their working and praying both.

See how clearly this connection comes out in our text. As His body here on earth, as those who are one with Him in heaven, they are now to do greater works than He had done; their success and their victories are to be greater than His. He mentiones two reasons for this. The one, because He was to go to the Father, to receive all power; the other, because they might now ask and expect all in His name. "Because I go unto the Father, *and*—notice this and—*and* whatever ye shall ask, I will do." His going to the Father would then bring the double blessing: they would ask and receive all in His name, and, as a consequence, would do the greater works. This first mention of prayer in our Savior's parting words therefore teaches us two most important lessons. He who would do the works of Jesus *must pray* in His name. He who would pray in His name *must work* in His name.

He who would work *must pray:* it is in prayer that the power for work is obtained. He who in faith would do the works that Jesus did, must pray in His name. As long as Jesus was here on earth, He Himself did the greatest works; devils that the disciples could not cast out, fled at His word. When He went to the Father, He was no longer here in the body to work directly. The disciples were now His body: all His work from the throne in heaven here on earth must and could be done through them. One might have thought that now that He was leaving the scene Himself, and could only work through commissioners, the works might be fewer and weaker. He assures us of the contrary: "*Verily, verily,* I say unto you, He that believeth on me, the works that I do shall he do also; and greater works shall he do than these." His approaching death was to be such a real breaking down and an ending of the power of sin; with the Resurrection the powers of the eternal life were so truly to take possession of the human body and to obtain supremacy over human life; with His ascension He was to receive the power to communicate the Holy Spirit so fully to His own; the union, the oneness between Himself on the throne and them on earth, was to be so intensely and divinely perfect, that He meant it as the literal truth: "Greater works than these shall he do; because I go unto the Father." And the issue proved how true it was. While Jesus during three years of personal labor on earth, gathered little more than five hundred disciples, and the most of them so feeble that they were but little credit to His cause, it was given to men like Peter and Paul manifestly to do greater things than He had done. From the throne He could do through them what He Himself in His humiliation could not yet do.

But there is one condition: "He that believeth on me . . . he shall do greater works, because I go unto the Father; *and whatsoever ye shall ask in my Name, that will I do.*" His going to the Father would give Him a new power to hear prayer. For the doing of the greater works, two things were needed: His going to the Father to receive all power, and our prayer in His name to receive all power from Him again. As He asks the Father, He receives and bestows on us the power of the new dispensation for the greater works; as we believe, and ask in His name, the power comes and takes possession of us to do the greater works.

Alas, how much working there is in the work of God in which there is little or nothing to be seen of the power to do anything like Christ's works, not to speak of greater works. There can be but one reason: the believing on Him, the believing prayer in His name, is so much wanting. O that every laborer and leader in church, or school, in the work of home philanthropy or foreign missions, might learn the lesson: prayer in the name of Jesus, the way to share in the mighty power that Jesus received of the Father for His people, and it is in this power alone that he who believes can do the greater works. To every complaint as to weakness or unfitness, as to difficulties or want of success, Jesus gives this one answer: "*He that believeth* on me . . . shall do greater works, because I go unto the Father. And *whatsoever ye shall ask* in my name, *that will I do.*" We must understand that the first and chief thing for every one who would do the work of Jesus, is to believe, and so to become like Him, the almighty One, and then to pray the prayer of faith in His name. Without this our work is but human and carnal; it may have some use in restraining sin, or preparing the way for blessing, but the real power is lacking. Effectual working first needs effectual prayer.

And now the second lesson: He who would pray *must work*. It is for power to work that prayer has such great promises:

it is in working that the power for the effectual prayer of faith will be gained. In these parting words of our blessed Lord we find that He no less than six times (John 14:13, 14; 15:7, 16; 16:23, 24) repeats those unlimited prayer promises that have so often awakened our anxious questionings as to their real meaning: "whatsoever," "anything," "what ye will," "ask and ye shall receive." How many believers have read these over with joy and hope, and in deep earnestness of soul have sought to plead them for their own need. And they have come out disappointed. The simple reason was this: they had torn the promise from its surroundings. The Lord gave the wonderful promise of the free use of His name with the Father in connection with the *doing of His works.* It is the disciple who gives himself wholly to live for Jesus' work and kingdom, for His will and honor, to whom the power will come to appropriate the promise. He who would grasp the promise when he wants something very special for himself will be disappointed, because he would make Jesus the servant of his own comfort. But to him who seeks to pray the effectual prayer of faith, because he needs it for the work of the Master, to him it will be given to learn it; because he has made himself the servant of his Lord's interests. Prayer not only teaches and strengthens to work: work teaches and strengthens to pray.

This is in perfect harmony with what holds good both in the natural and the spiritual world. Whoever has, to him shall be given; or, He who is faithful in a little, is faithful also in much. Let us with the small measure of grace already received, give ourselves to the Master for His work: work will be to us a real school of prayer. It was when Moses had to take full charge of a rebellious people that he felt the need, but also the courage, to speak boldly to God and to ask great things of Him (Exod. 23:12, 15, 18). As you give yourself entirely to God for His work, you will feel that nothing less than these great promises are what you need, that nothing less is what you may most confidently expect.

Believer in Jesus, you are called, you are appointed to do the works of Jesus, and even greater works, because He has gone to the Father to receive the power to do them in and through you.

"*Whatsoever* ye shall ask in my name, that *will I do.*" Give yourself, and live, to do the works of Christ, and you will learn to pray so as to obtain wonderful answers to prayer. Give yourself, and live, to pray, and you will learn to do the works He did, and greater works. With disciples full of faith in Himself and bold in prayer to ask great things, Christ can conquer the world.

* * * * *

O my Lord, I have this day again heard words from You that pass my comprehension. And yet I cannot do anything but in simple childlike faith take and keep them as Your gift to me too. You have said that in virtue of Your going to the Father, he who believes on You will do the works that You have done, and greater works. Lord, I worship You as the glorified One, and look for the fulfillment of Your promise. May my whole life just be one of continued believing in You. So purify and sanctify my heart, make it so tenderly susceptible of Yourself and Your love, that believing on You may be the very life it breathes.

And You have said that in virtue of Your going to the Father, whatsoever we ask, You will do. From Your throne of power You would make Your people share the power given You, and work through them as the members of Your body, in response to their believing prayers in Your name. Power in prayer with You, and power in work with men, is what You have promised Your people and me too.

Blessed Lord, forgive us that we have so little believed You and Your promise, and so little proved Your faithfulness in fulfilling it. O forgive us that we have so little honored Your all-prevailing name in heaven or on earth.

Lord, teach me to pray so that I may prove that Your name is indeed all-prevailing with God and men and devils. Yes, teach me so to work and so to pray that You can glorify Yourself in me as the Omnipotent One, and do Your great works through me too. Amen.

20 The Chief End of Prayer

I go unto the Father. And whatsoever ye shall ask in my name, that will I do, that the Father may be glorified in the Son.

John 14:13

That the Father may be glorified in the Son. It is to this end that Jesus on His throne in glory will do all we ask in His name. Every answer to prayer He gives will have this as its object: when there is no prospect of this object being obtained, He will not answer. It follows as a matter of course that this must be with us, as with Jesus, the essential in our petitions: the glory of the Father must be the aim and end, the very soul and life of our prayer.

It was so with Jesus when He was on earth. "I seek not mine own honor: I seek the honor of him that sent me." In such words we have the keynote of His life. In the first words of the high-prestly prayer He gives utterance to it: "Father . . . glorify thy son, *that the Son may glorify thee." "I glorified thee* on the earth . . . glorify thou me with thine own." The ground on which He asks to be taken up into the glory He had with the Father, is the twofold one: He has glorified Him on earth; He will still glorify Him in heaven. What He asks is only to enable Him to glorify the Father more. It is as we enter into sympathy with Jesus on this point, and gratify Him by making the Father's glory our chief object in prayer too, that our prayer cannot fail to get an answer. The beloved Son has said so distinctly that nothing will glorify the Father more than this, His doing what we ask; He will therefore not let any opportunity slip of securing this object. Let us make His aim ours: let the glory of the Father be the link between our asking and His doing: such prayer must prevail.

This word of Jesus comes indeed as a sharp two-edged sword, piercing even to the dividing of soul and spirit, and is quick to discern the thoughts and intents of the heart. Jesus in His prayers on earth, in His intercession in heaven, in His promise of an answer to our prayers from there, makes this His first object—the glory of His Father. Is it so with us too? Or are self-interest and self-will in large measure the strongest motives urging us to pray? If we cannot see that this is the case, can we not acknowledge that the distinct, conscious longing for the glory of the Father is not what animates our prayers? And yet it must be so.

It is not as if the believer does not at times desire it, but he has to mourn because he has attained so little. And he knows the reason of his failure too. It was because the separation between the spirit of daily life and the spirit of the hour of prayer was too wide. We begin to see that the desire for the glory of the Father is not something that we can awake and present to our Lord when we prepare ourselves to pray. No! it is only when the whole life, in all its parts, is given up to God's glory, that we can really pray to His glory too. "*Do all* to the glory of God," and, "*Ask all* to the glory of God"—these twin commands are inseparable. Obedience to the former is the secret of grace for the latter. A life to the glory of God is the condition of the prayers that Jesus can answer, "that the Father may be glorified."

This demand in connection with prevailing prayer—that it should be to the glory of God—is no more than right and natural. There is none glorious but the Lord: there is no glory but His, and what He bestows on His creatures. Creation exists to show His glory; all that is not for His glory is sin, and darkness, and death: it is only in the glorifying of God that the creatures can find glory. What the Son of Man did, to give Himself wholly, His whole life, to glorify the Father, is nothing but the simple duty of every redeemed one. And Christ's reward will be his too. Because He gave Himself so entirely to the glory of the Father, the Father crowned Him with glory and honor, giving the kingdom into His hands, with the power to ask what He will and, as Intercessor, to answer our prayers. And just as we become one with Christ in this, and as our prayer is part of a life utterly surrendered to God's glory, will the Savior be able to glorify the Father to us by the fulfillment of the promise: "Whatsoever ye shall ask . . . *that will I do.*"

To such a life, with God's glory our only aim, we cannot attain by any effort of our own. It is only in the man Christ Jesus that such a life is to be seen: in Him it is to be found for us. Yes, blessed be God! His life is our life. He gave *Himself* for us; He Himself is our life. The discovery, and the confession, and the denial of self, as usurping the place of God, of self-seeking and self-trusting, is essential, and yet is what we cannot accomplish in our own strength. It is the incoming and indwelling, the presence and the rule in the heart, of our Lord Jesus who glorified the Father on earth, and is now glorified with Him, that from that point on He might glorify Him in us—it is Jesus Himself coming in who can cast out all self-glorifying, and give us instead His own God-glorifying life and Spirit. It is Jesus who longs to glorify the Father in hearing our prayers, who will teach us to live and to pray to the glory of God.

And what motive, what power is there that can urge our slothful hearts to yield themselves to our Lord to work this in us? Surely nothing more is needed than a sight of how glorious, how alone worthy of glory the Father is. Let our faith learn in adoring worship to bow before Him, to ascribe to Him alone the kingdom, and the power, and the glory, to yield ourselves to dwell in His light as the ever-blessed, ever-loving One. Surely we shall be stirred to say, "To Him alone be glory." And we shall look to our Lord Jesus with new intensity of desire for a life that refuses to see or seek anything but the glory of God. When there is but little prayer that can be answered, the Father is not glorified. It is a duty, for the glory of God, to live and pray so that our prayer can be answered. For the sake of God's glory, let us learn to pray well.

What a humbling thought that so often there is earnest prayer for a child or a friend, for a work or a circle, in which the thought of our joy or our pleasure was far stronger than any yearnings for God's glory. No wonder that there are so many unanswered prayers: here we have the secret. God would not be glorified when that glory was not our object. He who would pray the prayer of faith, will have to give himself to live literally so that the Father in all things may be glorified in him. This must be his aim: without this there cannot be the prayer of faith. "How can you believe," said Jesus, "who receive glory of one another, and the glory that comes from the only God you do not seek?" All seeking of our own glory with men makes faith impossible: it is the deep, intense self-sacrifice that gives up its own glory, and seeks the glory of God alone, that wakens in the soul that spiritual susceptibility of the divine, which is faith. The surrender to God to seek His glory, and the expectation that He will show His glory in hearing us, are one at root: He who seeks God's glory will see it in the answer to his prayer, and he alone.

And how, we ask again, shall we attain it? Let us begin with confession. How little has the glory of God been an all-absorbing passion; how little our lives and our prayers have been full of it. How little have we lived in the likeness of the Son, and in sympathy with Him—for God and His glory alone. Let us take time, until the Holy Spirit shows it to us, and we see how wanting we have been in this. True knowledge and confession of sin are the sure path to deliverance.

And then let us look to Jesus. In Him we can see by what death we can glorify God. In death He glorified Him; through death He was glorified with Him. It is by dying, being dead to self and living to God, that we can glorify Him. And this— this death to self, this life to the glory of God—is what Jesus gives and lives in each one who can trust Him for it. Let nothing less than these—the desire, the decision to live only for the glory of the Father, even as Christ did; the acceptance of Him with His life and strength working it in us; the joyful assurance that we can live to the glory of God, because Christ lives in us—let this be the spirit of our daily life. Jesus stands surety for our living in this manner; the Holy Spirit is given, and is waiting to make it our experience, if we will only trust and let Him. Let us not hold back through unbelief, but confidently take as our watchword, All to the glory of God! The Father accepts the will, the sacrifice is well-pleasing; the Holy

Spirit will seal us within with the consciousness that we are living for God and His glory.

And then what quiet peace and power there will be in our prayers, as we know ourselves, through His grace, in perfect harmony with Him who says to us, when He promises to do what we ask: "That the Father may be glorified in the Son." With our whole being consciously yielding to the inspiration of the Word and Spirit, our desires will be no longer ours but His; their chief end the glory of God. With increasing liberty we shall be able in prayer to say: Father! You know, we ask it only for Your glory. And the condition of the answers to prayer, instead of being as a mountain we cannot climb, will only give us to greater confidence that we shall be heard, because we have seen that prayer has no higher beauty or blessedness than this, that it glorifies the Father. And the precious privilege of prayer will become doubly precious because it brings us into perfect union with the beloved Son in the wonderful partnership He proposes: "*You ask,* and *I do,* that the Father may be glorified in the Son."

* * * * *

Blessed Lord Jesus, I come again to You. Every lesson You give me convinces me more deeply how little I know to pray aright. But every lesson also inspires me with hope that You are going to teach me, that You are teaching me not only to know what prayer should be, but actually to pray as I ought. O my Lord! I look with courage to You, the Great Intercessor, who prayed and heard prayer, only that the Father could be glorified, to teach me to live and to pray to the glory of God.

Saviour, to this end I yield myself to You again. I would be nothing. I have given self, as already crucified with You, to the death. Through the Spirit, its workings are mortified and made dead; Your life and Your love of the Father are taking possession of me. A new longing begins to fill my soul, that every day, every hour, that in every prayer the glory of the Father may be everything to me. O my Lord, I am in Your school to learn this; teach it to me.

And God of glory, the Father of glory, my God and my Father, accept the desire of a child who has seen that Your glory is indeed alone worth living for. O Lord, show me Your glory. Let it overshadow me. Let it fill the temple of my heart. Let me dwell in it as revealed in Christ. And do fulfill in me Your own good pleasure, that Your child should find his glory in seeking the glory of his Father. Amen.

21 The All-inclusive Condition

If ye abide in me, and my words abide in you, ask what-soever ye will, and it shall be done unto you.

John 15:7

In all God's intercourse with us, the promise and its conditions are inseparable. If we fulfill the conditions, He fulfills the promise. What He is to be to us depends on what we are willing to be to Him. "Draw near to God, and he will draw near to you." And so in prayer the unlimited promise, *"Ask whatsoever ye will,"* has its one simple and natural condition, *"if ye abide in me."* It is Christ whom the Father always hears; God is *in Christ* and can only be reached by being in Him; to be in Him is the way to have our prayer heard; fully and wholly abiding in Him, we have the right to ask whatever we will, and also have the promise that it shall be done for us.

When we compare this promise with the experience of most believers, we are startled by a terrible discrepancy. Who can number the countless prayers that rise and bring no answer? The cause must be either that we do not fulfill the condition, or God does not fulfill the promise. Believers are not willing to admit either, and therefore have devised a way of escape from the dilemma. They put into the promise the qualifying clause our Savior did not put there—if it is God's will; and so maintain both God's integrity and their own. If we would only accept the verse and hold it fast as it stands, trusting to Christ to vindicate His truth, how God's Spirit would lead us to see the divine propriety of such a promise to those who really abide in Christ in the sense in which He means it, and to confess that the failure in the fulfilling the condition is the one sufficient explanation of unanswered prayer. And how the Holy Spirit would then make our feebleness in prayer one of the mightiest motives to urge us on to discover the secret, and obtain the blessing, of full abiding in Christ.

"If ye abide in me." As a Christian grows in grace and in the knowledge of the Lord Jesus, he is often surprised to find how the words of God grow too, in the new and deeper meaning with which they come to him. He can look back to the day when some word of God was opened up to him, and he rejoiced in the blessing he had found in it. After a time some deeper experience gave it a new meaning, and it was as if he never had seen what it contained. And yet once again, as he advanced in the Christian life, the same word stood before him as a mystery, until the Holy Spirit led him still deeper into its divine fullness. One of these ever-growing, never-exhausted words, opening up to us step by step the fullness of the divine life, is the Master's precious "abide in me." As the union of the branch with the vine is one of growth, never-ceasing growth and increase, so our abiding in Christ is a life process in which the divine life takes ever fuller and more complete possession of us. The young and feeble believer may be really abiding in Christ up to the measure of his light; it is he who reaches onward to the full abiding in the sense in which the Master understood the words, who inherits all the promises connected with it.

In the growing life of abiding in Christ, the first stage is that of faith. As the believer sees that, with all his feebleness, the command is really meant for him, his great aim is simply to believe that, as he knows he is in Christ, so now, notwithstanding unfaithfulness and failure, abiding in Christ is his immediate duty, and a blessing within his reach. He is especially occupied with the love, and power, and faithfulness of the Savior: he feels his one need to be believing.

It is not long before he sees that something more is needed. Obedience and faith must go together. It is not as if to the faith he has that obedience must be added, but faith must be made manifest in obedience. Faith is obedience at home and looking to the Master: obedience is faith going out to do His will. He sees how he has been more occupied with the privilege and the blessings of this abiding than with its duties and its fruit. There has been much of self and of self-will that has been unnoticed or tolerated: the peace which, as a young and feeble disciple, he could enjoy in believing goes from him; it is in practical obedience that the abiding must be maintained: "If ye keep my commandments, ye shall abide in my love." As before his great aim was through the *mind* and the truth it took hold of, to let the heart rest on Christ and His promises; so now, in this stage, his chief effort is to get his *will* united with the will of his Lord, and the heart and the life brought entirely under His rule.

And yet it is as if there is something wanting. The will and the heart are on Christ's side; he obeys and he loves his Lord. But still, why is it that the fleshly nature has yet so much power, that the spontaneous motions and emotions of the inmost being are not what they should be? The will does not approve or allow, but here is a region beyond control of the will. And why also, even when there is not so much of positive commission to condemn, why so much of omission, the deficiency of that beauty of holiness, that zeal of love, that conformity to Jesus and His death, in which the life of self is lost, and which is surely implied in the abiding as the Master meant it? There must surely be something in our abiding in Christ and Christ in us, which he has not yet experienced. It is so. Faith and obedience are but the pathway of blessing. Before giving us the parable of the vine and the branches, Jesus had distinctly told what the full blessing is to which faith and obedience are to lead. Three times over He had said, "If ye love me, keep my commandments," and spoken of the threefold blessing with which He would crown such obedient love. The Holy Spirit would come from the Father; the Son would manifest Himself; the Father and the Son would come and make their abode. It is as our faith grows into obedience, and in obedience and love our whole being goes out and clings to Christ, that our inner life becomes opened up, and the capacity is formed within of receiving the life, the spirit, of the glorified Jesus, as a distinct and conscious union with Christ and with the Father. The word is fulfilled in us: "In that day ye shall know that I am in my Father, and ye in me, and I in you." We understand how, just as Christ is in God, and God in Christ, one togehter not only in will and in love, but in identity of nature and life, because they exist in each other, so we are in Christ and Christ in us, in union not only of will and love, but of life and nature too.

It was after Jesus had spoken of our knowing through the Holy Spirit, that He is in the Father, and even so we in Him and He in us, that He said, "Abide in me, and I in you. Accept, consent to receive that divine life of union with Myself, in virtue of which, as you abide in Me, I also abide in you, even as I abide in the Father, so that your life is Mine and Mine is yours." This is the true abiding, the occupying of the position in which Christ can come and abide; so abiding in Him that the soul has come away from self to find that He has taken the place and become our life. It is the becoming as little children who have no care, and find their happiness in trusting and obeying the love that has done all for them.

To those who thus abide, the promise comes as their rightful heritage: Ask whatsoever ye will. It cannot be otherwise. Christ has full possession of them. Christ dwells in their love, their will, their life. Not only has their will been given up; Christ has entered it, and dwells and breathes in it by His Spirit. He whom the Father always hears, prays in them; they pray in Him: what they ask shall be done to them.

Beloved fellow-believer, let us confess that it is because we do not abide in Christ as He would have us, that the church is so impotent in the presence of the infidelity and worldliness and heathendom, in the midst of which the Lord is able to make her more than conqueror. Let us believe that He means what He promises, and accept the condemnation the confession implies.

But let us not be discouraged. The abiding of the branch in the Vine is a life of never-ceasing growth. The abiding, as the Master meant it, is within our reach, for He lives to give it to us. Let us but be ready to count all things loss, and to say, "Not as though I had already attained; I follow after, if that I may apprehend that for which I also am apprehended of Christ Jesus." Let us not be so much occupied with the abiding, as with Him to whom the abiding links us, and His fullness. Let it be Him, the whole Christ, in His obedience and humiliation, in His exaltation and power, in whom our soul moves and acts; He Himself will fulfill His promise in us.

And then as we abide, and grow more and more into the full abiding, let us exercise our right, the will to enter into all God's will. Obeying what that will commands, let us claim what it promises. Let us yield to the teaching of the Holy Spirit, to show each of us, according to his growth and measure, what the will of God is that we may claim in prayer. And let us rest content with nothing less than the personal experience of what Jesus gave when He said, "If ye abide in me . . . ask whatsoever ye will, it shall be done unto you."

* * * * *

Beloved Lord, teach me to take this promise anew in all its simplicity, and to be sure that the only measure of Your holy giving is our holy willing. Lord, let each word of this Your promise be made quick and powerful anew in my soul.

You say: *Abide in me!* O my Master, my Life, my All, I do abide in You. Give me to grow into all Your fullness. It is not the effort of faith seeking to cling to You, nor even the rest of faith, trusting You to keep me; it is not the obedience of the will, nor the keeping the commandments; but it is Yourself living in me as in the Father, that alone can satisfy me. It is Yourself, my Lord, no longer before me and above me, but one with me, and abiding in me; it is this I need, it is this I seek. It is this I trust You for.

You say: *Ask whatsoever ye will!* Lord! I know that the life of full, deep abiding will so renew and sanctify and strengthen the will that I shall have the light and the liberty to ask great things. Lord, let my will, dead in Your death, living in Your life, be bold and large in its petitions.

You say: *It shall be done.* O You who are the Amen, the Faithful and True Witness, give me in Yourself the joyous confidence that You will make this word yet more wonderfully true to me than ever, because it has not entered into the heart of man to conceive what God has prepared for those who love Him. Amen.

22 The Word and Prayer

If ye abide in me, and my words abide in you, *ask whatso-ever ye will, and it shall be done unto you.*

John 15:7

The vital connection between the word and prayer is one of the simplest and earliest lessons of the Christian life. As that newly-converted heathen put it: I pray—I speak to my father; I read—my Father speaks to me. Before prayer, it is God's word that prepares me for it, by revealing what the Father has requested me to ask. In prayer, God's word strengthens me by giving my faith its warrant and its plea. And after prayer, it is God's word that brings me the answer when I have prayed, for in it the Spirit gives me to hear the Father's voice. Prayer is not monologue but dialogue; God's voice in response to mine is its most essential part. Listening to God's voice is the secret of the assurance that He will listen to mine. "Incline thine ear, and hear"; "Give ear to me"; "Hearken to my voice"; are words that God speaks to man as well as man to God. His hearkening will depend on ours; the entrance His words find with me, will be the measure of the power of my words with Him. What God's words are to me, is the test of what He Himself is to me, and so of the uprightness of my desire after Him in prayer.

It is this connection between His word and our prayer that Jesus points to when He says, "If ye abide in me, *any my words abide in you,* ask whatsoever ye will, and it shall be done unto you." The deep importance of this truth becomes clear if we notice the other expression of which this one has taken the place. More than once Jesus had said, "Abide in me and *I in you.*" His abiding in us was the complement and the crown of our abiding in Him. But here, instead of "Ye in me *and I in you,*" He says, "Ye in me *and my words in you.*" His words abiding are the equivalent of Himself abiding.

What a view is opened up to us here of the place the words of God in Christ are to have in our spiritual life, and especially in our prayer. In a man's words *he reveals himself.* In his promises, *he gives himself away*; he binds himself to the one who receives his promise. In his commands he sets forth his will, seeks *to make himself master* of him whose obedience he claims, to guide and use him as if he were part of himself. It is through our words that spirit holds fellowship with spirit, that the spirit of one man passes over and transfers itself into another. It is through the words of a man, heard and accepted, and held fast and obeyed, that he can impart himself to another, although in a very relative and limited sense.

But when God, the infinite Being in whom everything is life and power, spirit and truth, in the very deepest meaning of the words—when God speaks Himself in His words, He does indeed give Himself, His Love and His Life, His Will and His power, to those who receive these words, in a reality passing comprehension. In every promise He puts *Himself* in our power to lay hold of and possess; in every command He puts *Himself* in our power for us to share with Him His Will, His Holiness, His Perfection. In God's Word He gives us Himself; His Word is nothing less than the Eternal Son, Christ Jesus. And so all of Christ's words are God's words, full of a divine quickening life and power. "The words that I have spoken unto you, are spirit and are life."

Those who have made the deaf and mute their study, tell us how much the power of speaking depends on that of hearing, and how the loss of hearing in children is followed by that of speaking too. This is true in a wider sense: as we hear, so we speak. This is true in the highest sense of our intercourse with God. To offer a prayer—to give utterance to certain wishes and to appeal to certain promises—is an easy thing, and can be learned by man through wisdom. But to pray in the Spirit, to speak words that reach and touch God, that affect and influence the powers of the unseen world—such praying, such speaking, depends entirely on our hearing God's voice. Just as far as we listen to the voice and language that God speaks, and in the words of God receive His thoughts, His mind, His life, into our heart, we shall learn to speak in the voice and language that God hears. It is the ear of the learner wakened morning by morning that prepares the tongue of the learned to speak to God as well as men, as it should be (Isa. 50:4).

This hearing the voice of God is something more than the thoughtful study of the Word. There may be a study and knowledge of the Word in which there is but little real fellowship with the living God. But there is also a reading of the Word, in the very presence of the Father, and under the leading of the Spirit, in which the Word comes to us in living power from God Himself; it is to us the very voice of the Father, a real personal fellowship with Him. It is the living voice of God that enters the heart, that brings blessing and strength, and awakens the response of a living faith that reaches the heart of God again.

It is on this hearing the voice that the power both to obey and believe depends. The chief thing is not to know *what* God has said we must do, but that *God Himself* says it to us. It is not the law, and not the book, not the knowledge of what is right, that works obedience, but the personal influence of God and His living fellowship. And even so it is not the knowledge of *what* God has promised, but the presence of *God Himself* as the Promiser, that awakens faith and trust in prayer. It is only in the full presence of God that disobedience and unbelief become impossible.

"If ye abide in me, and *my words abide in you,* ask whatsoever ye will, it shall be done unto you." We see what this means. In these words the Savior gives Himself. We must have the words *in us,* taken up into our will and life, reproduced in our disposition and conduct. We must have them *abiding* in us: our whole life one continued exposition of the words that are within, and filling us; the words revealing Christ within, and our life revealing Him without. It is as the words of Christ enter our very heart, become our life and influence it, that our words will enter His heart and influence Him. My prayer will depend on my life; what God's words are to me and in me, my words will be to God and in God. If I will do what God says He will do what I say.

How well the Old Testament saints understood this connection between God's words and ours, and how prayer with them was the loving response to what they had heard God speak! If the word were a promise, they counted *on God to do as He had spoken.* "Do as thou hast said"; "For thou, Lord, hast spoken it"; "According to thy promise"; "According to thy word": in such expressions they showed that what God spoke in promise was the root and the life of what they spoke in prayer. If the word was a command, they simply *did as the Lord had spoken.* "So Abram departed as the Lord had spoken." Their life was fellowship with God, the interchange of word and thought. What God apoke they heard and did; what they spoke God heard and did. In each word He speaks to us, the whole Christ gives Himself to fulfill it for us. For each word He asks no less that we give the whole man to keep that word, and to receive its fulfillment.

"If my words abide in you": the condition is simple and clear. In His words His will is revealed. As the words abide in me, His will rules me; my will becomes the empty vessel that His will fills, the willing instrument that His will wields; He fills my inner being. In the exercise of obedience and faith my will becomes ever stronger, and is brought into deeper inner harmony with Him. He can fully trust it to will nothing but what He wills; He is not afraid to give the promise, "If my words abide in you, ask whatsoever ye will, and it shall be done unto you." To all who believe it, and act upon it, He will make it literally true.

Disciples of Christ, is it not becoming more and more clear to us that while we have been excusing our unanswered prayers, our impotence in prayer, with a fancied submission to God's wisdom and will, the real reason has been that our own feeble life has been the cause of our feeble prayers. Nothing can make strong men but the word coming to us from God's mouth: by that we must live. It is the word of Christ, loved, lived in, abiding in us, becoming through obedience and action part of our being, that makes us one with Christ, that fits us spiritually for touching, for taking hold of God. All that is of the world passes away; he who does the will of God abides forever. O let us yield heart and life to the words of Christ, the words in which He ever gives Himself, the personal living Savior, and His promise will be our rich experience: "If ye abide in me, and my words abide in you, ask whatsoever ye will, and it shall be done unto you."

* * * * *

Blessed Lord, Your lesson this day has again shown me my folly. I see how it is that my prayer has not been more believing and prevailing. I was more occupied with my speaking to You than Your speaking to me. I did not understand that the secret of faith is this: there can be only so much faith as there is of the living Word dwelling in the soul.

And Your word had taught me so clearly: Let every man be swift to hear, slow to speak; do not let Your heart be hasty to utter anything before God. Lord, teach me that it is only with Your word taken up into my life that my words can be taken into Your heart; that Your word, if it is a living power within me, will be a living power with You; what Your mouth has spoken Your hand will perform.

Lord, deliver me from the uncircumcised ear. Give me the opened ear of the learner, wakened morning by morning to hear the Father's voice. Even as You only spoke what You heard, may my speaking be the echo of Your speaking to me. "When Moses went into the tabernacle to speak with him, he heard the voice of One speaking unto him from off the mercy-seat." Lord, may it be so with me too. Let a life and character bearing the one mark, that Your words abide and are seen in it, be the preparation for the full blessing: "Ask whatsoever ye will, and it shall be done unto you." Amen.

23 *Obedience the Path to Power in Prayer*

Ye did not choose me, but I chose you, and appointed you, that ye should go and bear fruit, and that your fruit should abide; that whatsoever ye shall ask *of the Father in my name, he may give it you*

John 15:16

The fervent effectual prayer of a righteous man availeth much.

James 5:16

The promise of the Father's giving whatever we ask is here once again renewed, in such a connection as to show us to whom it is that such wonderful influence in the council chamber of the Most High is to be granted. "I chose you," the Master says, "and appointed you, that ye should go and bear fruit, and that your fruit should abide"; and then He adds, *to the end "that* whatsoever ye," the fruit-bearing ones, "shall ask of the Father in my name, he may give it you." This is nothing but the fuller expression of what He had spoken in the words, "If ye abide in me." He had spoken of the object of this abiding as the bearing fruit, "more fruit," "much fruit": in this was God to be glorified, and the mark of discipleship seen. No wonder that He now adds that where the reality of the abiding is seen in fruit abounding and abiding, this would be the qualification for praying so as to obtain what we ask. Entire consecration to the fulfillment of our calling is the condition of effectual prayer, the key to the unlimited blessings of Christ's wonderful prayer promises.

There are Christians who fear that such a statement is at variance with the doctrine of free grace. But surely not of free

grace rightly understood, nor with so many express statements of God's blessed word. Take the words of John
(1 John 3:19-22): "Let us love . . . in deed and truth. *Hereby*
shall we assure our heart before him . . . and whatsoever we
ask we receive of him, *because* we keep his commandments
and do the things that are pleasing in his sight." Or take the
oft-quoted words of James: "The fervent effectual prayer of a
righteous man availeth much"; that is, of a man of whom,
according to the definition of the Holy Spirit, it can be said,
"He that doeth righteousness, is righteous even as he is righteous." Mark the spirit of so many of the Psalms, with their
confident appeal to the integrity and righteousness of the
supplicant. In Ps. 18 David says: "The LORD rewarded me according to my righteousness; according to the cleanness of
my hands hath he recompensed me. . . . I was perfect with
him, and I kept myself from mine inquity. Therefore hath the
LORD recompensed me according to my righteousness.(Ps.
18:20-26. See also Ps. 7:3-5; 15:1, 2; 17:3, 6; 26:1-6; 119; 121,
153). If we carefully consider such utterances in the light of
the New Testament, we shall find them in perfect harmony
with the explicit teaching of the Savior's parting words: "*If ye
keep* my commandments, ye shall abide in my love"; "Ye are
my friends *if ye do* what I command you." The word is indeed
meant literally: "I appointed you that ye should go and bear
fruit, *that*," then, "whatsoever ye shall ask of the Father in
my name, he may give it you."

Let us seek to enter into the spirit of what the Savior teaches
us here. There is a danger in our evangelical religion of looking too much at what it offers from one side, as a certain
experience to be obtained in prayer and faith. There is another side that God's word speaks of very strongly, that of
obedience as the only path to blessing. What we need is to
realize that in our relationship to the Infinite Being whom we
call God, who has created and redeemed us, the first senti-
ment that ought to animate us is that of subjection: the surrender to His supremacy, His glory, His will, His pleasure,
ought to be the first and uppermost thought of our life. The
question is not how we are to obtain and enjoy His favor, for
in this main thing may still be self. But what this Being in

the very nature of things rightfully claims, and is infinitely and unspeakably worthy of, is that His glory and pleasure should be my one object. Surrender to His perfect and blessed will, a life of service and obedience, is the beauty and the charm of heaven. Service and obedience, these were the thoughts that were uppermost in the mind of the Son when He dwelt on earth. Service and obedience, these must become with us the chief objects of desire and aim, more so than rest or light, or joy or strength: in them we shall find the path to all the higher blessedness that awaits us.

Just note what a prominent place the Master gives it, not only in this 15th chapter, in connection with the abiding, but in the 14th, where He speaks of the indwelling of the Three-One God. In verse 15 we read: "*If ye* love me, ye will *keep my commandments,*" and the Spirit will be given of the Father. Then verse 21: "He that hath *my commandments, and keepeth them,* he it is that loveth me"; and he shall have the special love of my Father resting on him, and the special manifestation of Myself. Then again, verse 23, one of the highest of all the exceeding great and precious promises: "If a man love me *he will keep my word:* and the Father and I will come unto him and make our abode with him." Could words put it more clearly that obedience is the way to indwelling of the Spirit, to His revealing the Son within us, and to His again preparing us to be the abode, the home of the Father? The indwelling of the Three-One God is the heritage of those who obey. Obedience and faith are but two aspects of one act— surrender to God and His will. As faith strengthens for obedience, it is in turn strengthened by it: faith is made perfect by works. It is to be feared that often our efforts to believe have been unavailing because we have not taken up the only position in which a large faith is legitimate or possible, that of entire surrender to the honor and the will of God. It is the man who is entirely consecrated to God and His will who will find the power come to claim everything that his God has promised to be for him.

The application of this in the school of prayer is very simple, but very solemn. "I chose you," the Master says, "and appointed you that ye should go and bear fruit," much fruit

(vv. 5, 8), "and that your fruit should abide," that your life might be one of abiding fruit and abiding fruitfulness, "*that*" thus, as fruitful branches abiding in me, "whatsoever ye shall ask of the Father in my name, He may give it you." O how often we have sought to be able to pray the effectual prayer for much grace to bear fruit, and have wondered why the answer did not come. It was because we were reversing the Master's order. We wanted to have the comfort and the joy and the strength first, that we might do the work easily and without any feeling of difficulty and self-sacrifice. And He wanted us in faith, without asking whether we felt weak or strong, whether the work was hard or easy, in the obedience of faith to do what He said: the path of fruit-bearing would have led us to the place and the power of prevailing prayer. Obedience is the only path that leads to the glory of God. It is not obedience instead of faith, nor obedience to supply the shortcomings of faith; no, but faith's obedience gives access to all the blessings our God has for us. The baptism of the Spirit (14:16), the manifestation of the Son (14:21), the indwelling of the Father (14:23), the abiding in Christ's love (15:10), the privilege of His holy friendship (15:14), and the power of all-prevailing prayer (15:16)—all wait for the obedient.

Let us take the lessons home. Now we know the reason why we have not had power in faith to pray prevailingly. Our life was not as it should have been: simple downright obedience, abiding fruitfulness, was not its chief mark. And with our whole heart we approve of the divine appointment: men to whom God is to give such influence in the rule of the world, as at their request to do what otherwise would not have taken place, men whose will is to guide the path in which God's will is to work, must be men who have themselves learned obedience, whose loyalty and submission to authority must be above all suspicion. Our whole soul approves the law: obedience and fruit-bearing, the path to prevailing prayer. And with shame we acknowledge how little our lives have yet borne this stamp.

Let us yield ourselves to take up the appointment the Savior gives us. Let us study His relation to us as Master. Let us seek no more with each new day to think in the first place of comfort, or joy, or blessing. Let the first thought be: I belong to the Master. Every moment and every movement I must act as His property, as a part of Himself, as one who only seeks to know and do His will. A servant, a slave of Jesus Christ—let this be the spirit that animates me. If He says, "No longer do I call you servants, but I have called you friends," let us accept the place of friends: "Ye are my friends if ye do the things which I command you."

The one thing He commands us as His branches is to bear fruit. Let us live to bless others, to testify of the life and the love there is in Jesus. Let us in faith and obedience give our whole life to that which Jesus chose us for and appointed us to—fruit-bearing. As we think of His electing us to this, and take up our appointment as coming from Him who always gives all He demands, we shall grow strong in the confidence that a life of fruit-bearing, abounding and abiding, is within our reach. And we shall understand why this fruit-bearing alone can be the path to the place of all-prevailing prayer. It is the man who, in obedience to the Christ of God, is proving that he is doing what his Lord wills, for whom the Father will do whatever He will: "Whatsoever we ask we receive, because we keep his commandments, and do the things that are pleasing in his sight."

*   *   *   *   *

Blessed Master! teach me to apprehend fully what I only partly realize, that it is only through the will of God, accepted and acted out in obedience to His commands, that we obtain the power to grasp His will in His promises and fully appropriate them in our prayers. And teach me that it is in the path of fruit-bearing that the deeper growth of the branch into the Vine can be perfected, and we attain to that perfect oneness with Yourself in which we ask whatever we will.

Or Lord, reveal to us, we pray, how with all the hosts of heaven, and with Yourself the Son on earth, and with all the men of faith who have glorified You on earth, *obedience to God is our highest privilege, because it gives access to oneness with Himself in that which is His highest glory—His all-perfect will.* Your commandments and bearing fruit according to Your will, our spiritual nature will grow up to the full stature of the perfect man, with power to ask and to receive whatever we will.

O Lord Jesus, reveal Yourself to us, and the reality of Your purpose and Your power to make these Your wonderful promises the daily experience of all who utterly yield themselves to You and Your words. Amen.

24 The All-Prevailing Plea

Whatsoever ye shall ask in my name, *that will I do. If ye shall ask me anything* in my name, *that will I do. That whatsoever ye shall ask the Father* in my name, *He may give it you. Verily, verily, I say unto you, If ye shall ask anything of the Father, he will give it you* in my name. *Hitherto ye have asked nothing* in my name: *ask, and ye shall receive. In that day ye shall ask* in my name.

John 14:13, 14; 15:16; 16:23, 24, 26

Up to this point the disciples had not asked in the name of Christ, nor had He Himself ever used the expression. The nearest approach is, "met together in my name." Here is His parting words, He repeats the word unceasingly in connection with those promises of unlimited meaning, "Whatsoever," "Anything," "What Ye Will," to teach them and us that His name is our only, but also our all-sufficient plea. The power of prayer and the answer depend on the right use of the name.

What is a person's name? That word or expression in which the person is called up or represented to us. When I mention or hear a name, it calls up before me the whole man, what I know of him, and also the impression he has made on me. The name of a king includes his honor, his power, his kingdom. His name is the symbol of his power. So each name of God embodies and represents some part of the glory of the Unseen One. And the name of Christ is the expression of all He has done and all He is and lives to do as our Mediator.

And what is it to do a thing in the name of another? It is to come with power and authority of that other, as his representative and substitute. We know how such a use of another's name always supposes a community of interest. No one would give another the free use of his name without first being assured that his honor and interest were as safe as with himself.

And what is it when Jesus gives us power over His name, the free use of it, with the assurance that whatever we ask in it will be given to us? The ordinary comparison of one person giving another, on some special occasion, the liberty to ask something in his name, comes altogether short here—Jesus solemnly gives to *all* His disciples a general and unlimited power of the free use of His name at *all* times for *all* they desire. He could not do this if He did not know that He could trust us with His interests, that His honor would be safe in our hands. The free use of the name of another is always the token of great confidence, of close union. He who gives his name to another stands aside, to let that other act for him; he who takes the name of another, gives up his own as of no value. When I go in the name of another, I deny myself, I take not only his name, but himself and what he is, instead of myself and what I am.

Such a use of the name of a person may be in virtue of *a legal union*. A merchant leaving his home and business, gives his chief clerk a general power by which he can draw thousands of pounds in the merchant's name. The clerk does this, not for himself, but only in the interests of the business. It is because the merchant knows and trusts him as wholly devoted to his interest and business, that he dares put his name and property at his command. When the Lord Jesus went to heaven, He left His work, the management of His kingdom on earth, in the hands of His servants. He could not do otherwise than also give them His name to draw all the supplies they needed for the due conduct of His business. And they have the spiritual power to avail themselves of the name of Jesus just to the extent to which they yield themselves to live only for the interests and the work of the Master. The use of the name always supposes the surrender of our interests to Him whom we represent.

Or such a use of the name may be in virtue of a *life union*. In the case of the merchant and his clerk, the union is temporary. But we know how oneness of life on earth gives one-ness of name: a child has the father's name because he has his life. And often the child of a good father has been honored or helped by others for the sake of the name he bore. But this would not last long if it were found that it was only a name, and that the father's character was wanting. The name and the character or spirit must be in harmony. When such is the case, the child will have a double claim on the father's friends: the character secures and increases the love and esteem ren-dered first for the name's sake. So it is with Jesus and the believer: we are one, we have one life, one Spirit with Him; for this reason we may come in His name. Our power in using that name, whether with God, or men, or devils, *depends on the measure of our spiritual life-union.* The use of the name rests on the unity of life; the name and the Spirit of Jesus are one.[1]

Or the union that empowers to the use of the name may be *the union of love.* When a bride whose life has been one of poverty, becomes united to the bridegroom, she gives up her own name, to be called by his, and has now the full right to use it. She purchases in his name, and that name is not refused. And this is done because the bridegroom has chosen her for himself, counting on her to care for his interests: they are now one. And so the heavenly Bridegroom could do noth-ing less; having loved us and made us one with Himself, what could He do but give those who bear His name the right to present it before the Father, or to come with it to Himself for all they need. And there is no one who gives himself really to live in the name of Jesus, who does not receive in ever-in-creasing measure the spiritual capacity to ask and receive in that name what he will. The bearing of the name of another supposes my having given up my own, and with it my own

[1]"Whatsoever ye shall ask in my name," that is, in my nature; for things with God are called according to their nature. We ask in Christ's name, not when at the end of some request we say, 'This I ask in the name of Jesus Christ.' but when we pray *according to His nature,* which is love, which seeketh not its own, but only the will of God and the good of all creatures. Such asking is the cry of His own Spirit in our hearts.—JUKES, *The New Man.*

independent life; but then, as surely, my possession of all there is in the name I have taken instead of my own.

Such illustrations show us how defective the common view is of a messenger sent to ask in the name of another, or a guilty one appealing to the name of a surety. No, Jesus Himself is with the Father; it is not an absent one in whose name we come. Even when we pray to Jesus Himself, it must be in His name. The name represents the person; to ask in the name is to ask in full union of interest and life and love with Himself, as one who lives in and for Him. Let the name of Jesus only have undivided supremacy in my heart and life, my faith will grow to the assurance that what I ask in that name cannot be refused. The name and power of asking go together: when the name of Jesus has become the power that rules my life, this power in prayer with God will be seen too.

We see therefore that everything depends on our own relation to the name: the power it has on my life is the power it will have in my prayers. There is more than one expression in Scripture that can make this clear to us. When it says, "*Do all* in the name of the Lord Jesus," we see how this is the counterpart of the other, "*Ask all.*" To do all and to ask all in His name go together. When we read, "We shall walk in the name of our God," we see how the power of the name must rule in the whole life; only then will it have power in prayer. It is not to the lips but to the life God looks to see what the name is to us. When Scripture speaks of "men who have given their lives for the name of the Lord Jesus," or of one "ready to die for the name of the Lord Jesus," we see what our relation to the name must be: when it is everything to me, it will obtain everything for me. If I let it have all I have, it will let me have all it has.

"Whatsoever ye shall ask in my name, that will I do." Jesus means the promise literally. Christians have sought to limit it: it looked too free; it was hardly safe to trust man so unconditionally. We did not understand that the word "in my name" is its own safeguard. It is a spiritual power that no one can use further than he has the capacity for, by his living and acting in that name. As we bear that name before men, we have power to use it before God. Let us plead for God's Holy

Spirit to show us what the name means, and its right use. It is through the Spirit that the name, which is above every name in heaven, will take the place of supremacy in our heart and life too.

Disciples of Jesus, let the lessons of this day enter deep into your hearts. The Master tells us we are to pray only in His name; whatsoever you ask will be given. Heaven is set open to you; the treasures and power of the world of spirit are placed at your disposal on behalf of men around you. O come, and let us learn to pray in the name of Jesus. As to the disciples, He says to us, "Hitherto ye have not asked in my name: ask, and ye shall receive." Let each disciple of Jesus seek to avail himself of the rights of his royal priesthood, and use the power placed at his disposal for his circle and his work. Let Christians awake and hear the message: your prayer can obtain what otherwise will be withheld, can accomplish what otherwise remains undone. O awake, and use the name of Jesus to open the treasures of heaven for this perishing world. Learn as the servants of the King to use His name: "Whatsoever ye shall ask in my name, That Will I do."

* * * * *

Blessed Lord! it is as if each lesson You give me has such fullness and depths of meaning, that if I can only learn that one, I shall know how to pray aright. This day I felt again as if I needed but one prayer every day: Lord! teach me what it is to pray in Your name. Teach me so to live and act, to walk and speak, as to do all in the name of Jesus, that my prayer cannot be anything else but in that blessed name too.

And teach me, Lord! to hold fast the precious promise that whatsoever we ask in Your name, You will do, the Father will give. Though I do not yet fully understand, and still less have fully attained, the wondrous union You mean when You say, in My name, I would yet hold fast the promise until it fills my heart with the undoubting assurance: anything in the name of Jesus.

On my Lord, let Your Holy Spirit teach me this. You did say of Him, "The Comforter, whom the Father shall send in my name." He knows what it is to be from heaven in Your name, to reveal and to honor the power of that name in Your servants, to use that name alone, and so to glorify You. Lord Jesus, let Your Spirit dwell in me, and fill me. I would, I do yield my whole being to His rule and leading. Your name and Your Spirit are one; through Him Your name will be the strength of my life and my prayer. Then I shall be able for Your name's sake to forsake all, in Your name to speak to men and to God, and to prove that this is indeed the name above every name.

Lord Jesus, O teach me by Your Holy Spirit to pray in Your name. Amen.

25 The Holy Spirit and Prayer

In that day *ye shall ask me no question. Verily, verily I say unto you,* If ye shall ask *anything of the Father he will give it you in my name.* Hitherto *have ye asked nothing in my name: ask, and* ye shall receive, *that your joy may be full.* In that day *ye shall ask in my name: and I say not unto you that I will pray the Father for you; for the Father himself loveth you.*

John 16:23-26

Praying in the Holy Spirit, keep yourselves in the love of God.

Jude 20, 21

The words of John (1 John 2:12-14) to little children, to young men, and to fathers, suggest the thought that there often are in the Christian life three great stages of experience. The first, that of the new-born child, with the assurance and the joy of forgiveness. The second, the transition stage of struggle and growth in knowledge and strength: young men growing strong, God's word doing its work in them and giving them victory over the Evil One. And then the final stage of maturity and ripeness: the fathers, who have entered deeply into the knowledge and fellowship of the Eternal One.

In Christ's teaching on prayer there appears to be three stages in the prayer life, somewhat analogous. In the Sermon on the Mount we have the initial stage: His teaching is all comprised in one word, Father. Pray to your Father, your Father sees, hears, knows, and will reward: *how much more* than any earthly father! Only be childlike and trustful. Then later on something like the transition stage of conflict and conquest appears in words like these: "This sort goeth not out but by fasting and prayer"; "Shall not God avenge his own elect who cry day and night unto Him?" And then we have in the parting words, a higher stage. The children have become men: they are now the Master's friends, from whom He has no secrets, to whom He says, "All things that I heard from my Father I made known unto you"; and to whom, in the oft-repeated "whatsoever ye will," He hands over the keys of the kingdom. Now the time has come for the power of prayer in His name to be proved.

The contrast between this final stage and the previous preparatory ones our Savior marks most distinctly in the words we are to meditate on. "*Hitherto* ye have asked nothing in my name"; "*At that day* ye shall ask in my name." We know what "at that day" means. It is the day of the outpouring of the Holy Spirit. The great work Christ was to do on the cross, the mighty power and the complete victory to be manifested in His resurrection and ascension, were to issue in the coming down from heaven, as never before, of the glory of God to dwell in men. The Spirit of the glorified Jesus was to come and be the life of His disciples. And one of the marks of that wonderful spirit-dispensation was to be a power in prayer up to this time unknown—prayer in the name of Jesus, asking and obtaining whatever they would, is to be the manifestation of the reality of the Spirit's indwelling.

To understand how the coming of the Holy Spirit was indeed to begin a new epoch in the prayer world, we must remember who He is, what His work, and what the significance of His not being given until Jesus was glorified. It is in the Spirit that God exists, for He is Spirit. It is in the Spirit that the Son was begotten of the Father: it is in the fellowship of the Spirit that the Father and the Son are one. The eternal never-ceasing giving to the Son, which is the Father's prerogative, and the eternal asking and receiving, which is the Son's right and blessedness—it is through the Spirit that this communion of life and love is maintained. It has been so from all eternity. It is so especially now, when the Son as mediator ever lives to pray. The great work that Jesus began on earth of reconciling in His own body God and man, He carries on in heaven. To accomplish this He took up into His own person the conflict between God's righteousness and our sin. On the cross He once for all ended the struggle in His own body. And then He ascended to heaven, that from there He might in each member of His body carry out the deliverance and manifest the victory He had obtained. It is to this that He ever lives to pray: in His unceasing intercession He places Himself in living fellowship with the unceasing prayer of His redeemed ones. Or rather, it is His unceasing intercession that shows itself in their prayers, and gives them a power they never had before.

And He does this through the Holy Spirit. The Holy Spirit, the Spirit of the glorified Jesus, was not (John 7:39), could not be, until He had been glorified. This gift of the Father was something distinctively new, entirely different from what Old Testament saints had known. The work that the blood effected in heaven when Christ entered within the veil, was something so true and new, the redemption of our human nature into fellowship with His resurrection power and His exaltation glory was so intensely real, the taking up of our humanity in Christ into the life of the Three-One God was an event of such inconceivable significance, that the Holy Spirit, who had to come from Christ's exalted humanity to testify in our hearts of what Christ had accomplished, was indeed no longer only what He had been in the Old Testament. It was literally true that the Holy Spirit was not yet, for Christ was not yet glorified. He came now first as the Spirit of the glorified Jesus. Even as the Son, who was from eternity God, had entered upon a new existence as man, and returned to heaven with what He did not have before, so the blessed Spirit, whom the Son, on His ascension, received from the Father (Acts 2:33) into His glorified humanity, came to us with a new life, which He had not previously communicated. Under the Old Testament He was invoked as the Spirit of God: at Pentecost He descended as the Spirit of the glorified Jesus, bringing down and communicating to us the full fruit and power of the accomplished redemption.

It is in the intercession of Christ that the continued efficacy and application of His redemption is maintained. And it is through the Holy Spirit descending from Christ to us that we are drawn up into the great stream of His ever-ascending prayers. The Spirit prays for us without words: in the depths of a heart where even thoughts are at times formless, the Spirit takes us up into the wonderful flow of the life of the Three-One God. Through the Spirit, Christ's prayers become ours, and ours are made His: we ask what we will, and it is given to us. We then understand from experience, "Hitherto ye have not asked in my name." "*At that day* ye shall ask in my name."

Brother, what we need to pray in the name of Christ, to ask that we may receive that our joy may be full, is the baptism of this Holy Spirit. This is more than the Spirit of God under the Old Testament. This is more than the Spirit of conversion and regeneration the disciples had before Pentecost. This is more than the Spirit with a measure of His influence and working. This is the Holy Spirit, the Spirit of the glorified Jesus in His exaltation-power, coming on us as the Spirit of the indwelling Jesus, revealing the Son and the Father within. (John 14:16-23). It is when this Spirit is the Spirit not of our hours of prayer, but of our whole life and walk, when this Spirit glorifies Jesus in us by revealing the completeness of His work, and makes us wholly one with Him and like Him, that we can pray in His name, because we are in very deed one with Him. Then it is that we have that immediateness of access to the Father of which Jesus says, "I say not that I will pray the Father for you." Oh, we need to understand and believe that to be filled with this, the Spirit of the glorified One, is the one need of God's believing people. Then shall we realize what it is, "with all prayer and supplication to be praying at all seasons in the Spirit," and what it is, "praying in the Holy Ghost, to keep ourselves in the love of God." "*At that day* ye shall ask in my name."

So once again the lesson comes: What our prayer avails, depends on what we are and what our life is. It is living in the name of Christ that is the secret of praying in the name of Christ; living in the Spirit that fits for praying in the Spirit. It is abiding in Christ that gives the right and power to ask what we will: the extent of the abiding is the exact measure of the power in prayer. It is the Spirit dwelling within us that prays, not in words and thoughts always, but in a breathing and a being deeper than utterance. Just so much as there is of Christ's Spirit in us, is the real prayer. Our lives, our lives, O let our lives be full of Christ, and full of His Spirit, and the wonderfully unlimited promises to our prayer will no longer appear strange. "Hitherto ye have asked nothing in my name. Ask, and ye shall receive, that your joy may be full. At that day ye shall ask in my name. Verily, verily,I say unto you, Whatsoever ye shall ask the Father in my name, He will give it you."

*   *   *   *   *

O my God, in holy awe I bow before You, the Three in One. Again I have seen how the mystery of prayer is the mystery of the Holy Trinity. I adore the Father who ever hears, and the Son who ever lives to pray, and the Holy Spirit, proceeding from the Father and the Son, to lift us up into the fellowship of that ever-blessed, never-ceasing asking and receiving. I bow, my God, in adoring worship, before the infinite condescension that, through the Holy Spirit, takes us and our prayers into the divine life, and its fellowship of love.

O my blessed Lord Jesus, teach me to understand Your lesson, that it is the indwelling Spirit, streaming from You, uniting to You, who is the Spirit of prayer. Teach me what it is as an empty, wholly consecrated vessel, to yield myself to His being my life. Teach me to honor and trust Him, as a living person, to lead my life and my prayer. Teach me especially in prayer to wait in holy silence, and give Him place to breathe within me His unmutterable intercession. And teach me that through Him it is possible to pray without ceasing, and to pray without failing, because He makes me partaker of the never-ceasing and never-failing intercession in which You, the Son, appear before the Father. Yea, Lord, fulfill in me Your promise, "At that day ye shall ask in my name. Verily, verily, I say unto you, Whatsoever ye shall ask the Father in my name, that will he give." Amen.

26 Christit the Intercessor

But I have prayed for thee, that thy faith fail not.

Luke 22:32

I say not unto you, that I will pray the Father for you

John 16:26

He ever liveth to make intercession

Hebrews 7:25

All growth in the spiritual life is connected with the clearer insight into what Jesus is to us. The more I realize that Christ must be all to me and in me, that all in Christ is indeed for me, the more I learn to live the real life of faith which, dying to self, lives wholly in Christ. The Christian life is no longer the vain struggle to live right, but the resting in Christ and finding strength in Him as our life, to fight the fight and gain the victory of faith. This is especially true of the life of prayer. As it also comes under the law of faith alone, and is seen in the light of the fullness and completeness there is in Jesus, the believer understands that it need no longer be a matter of strain or anxious care, but an experience of what Christ will do for him and in him—a participation in that life of Christ which, as on earth, so in heaven, ever ascends to the Father as prayer. And he begins to pray, not only trusting in the merits of Jesus, or in the intercession by which our unworthy prayers are made acceptable, but in that near and close union in virtue of which He prays in us and we in Him. The whole of salvation is Christ Himself: He has given Himself to us; He Himself lives in us. Because He prays, we pray too. As the disciples, when they saw Jesus pray, asked Him to make them partakers of what He knew of prayer, so we, now that we see Him as intercessor on the throne, know that He makes us participate with Himself in the life of prayer.

How clearly this comes out in the last night of His life. In His high-priestly prayer (John 17), He shows us how and what He has to pray to the Father, and will pray when once ascended to heaven. And yet He had in His parting address so repeatedly also connected His going to the Father with *their* new life of prayer. The two would be ultimately connected: His entrance on the work of His eternal intercession *would be the commencement and the power of their new prayer life in His name.* It is the sight of Jesus in His intercession that gives us power to pray in His name: all right and power of prayer is Christ; He makes us share in His intercession.

To understand this, think first of *His intercession:* He ever lives to make intercession. The work of Christ on earth as priest was but a beginning. It was as Aaron He shed His blood; it is as Melchizedek that He now lives within the veil to continue His work after the power of the eternal life. As Melchizedek is more glorious than Aaron, so it is in the work of intercession that the atonement has its true power and glory. "It is Christ Jesus that died: *yea more . . .* who is at the right hand of God, who also maketh intercession for us." That intercession is an intense reality, a work that is absolutely necessary, and without which the continued application of redemption cannot take place. In the incarnation and resurrection of Jesus the wondrous reconciliation took place, by which man became partaker of the divine life and blessedness. But the real personal appropriation of this reconcilation in each of His members here below cannot take place without the unceasing exercise of His divine power by the head in heaven. In all conversion and sanctification, in every victory over sin and the world, there is a real putting forth of the power of Him who is mighty to save. And this exercise of His power takes place only through His prayer: He asks of the Father, and receives from the Father. "*He is able* to save to the uttermost, *because* he ever liveth to make intercession." There is not a need of His people but He receives in intercession what the Godhead has to give: His mediation on the throne is as real and indispensable as on the cross. Nothing takes place without His intercession: it engages all His time and powers, is His unceasing occupation at the right hand of the Father.

And we participate not only in the benefits of this His work, but in the work itself because we are His body. Body and members are one: "The head cannot say to the feet, I have no need of thee." We share with Jesus in all He is and has: "The glory which thou gavest me, I have given them" We are partakers of His life, His righteousness, His work: we share with Him in His intercession too; it is not a work He does without us.

We do this because we are partakers of His life. "Christ is our life"; "No longer I, but Christ liveth in me." The life in Him and in us is identical, one and the same. His life in heaven is an *ever-praying* life. When it descends and takes possession of us, it does not lose its character; in us too it is the *ever-praying* life. When it descends and takes possession of us, it does not lose its character; in us too it is the *ever-praying* life—a life that without ceasing asks and receives from God. It is not as if there were two separate currents of prayer rising upward, one from Him, and one from His people. No, but the substantial life union is also prayer-union: what He prays passes through us, what we pray passes through Him. He is the angel with the golden censer: "Unto him there was given much incense," the secret of acceptable prayer, "that he should add it unto the prayers of all the saints upon the golden altar." We live, we abide in Him, the Interceding One.

The only-begotten is the only one who has the right to pray: to Him alone it was said, "Ask, and it shall be given thee." As in all other things the fullness dwells in Him, so the true prayer fullness too; He alone has the power of prayer. And just as the growth of the spiritual life consists in the clearer insight that all the treasures are *in Him*, and that we too are *in Him*, to receive each moment what we possess in Him, grace for grace, so with the prayer life too. Our faith in the intercession of Jesus must not only be that He prays in our stead, when we do not or cannot pray, but that, as the Author of our life and our faith, He draws us on to pray in unison with Himself. Our prayer must be a work of faith in this sense too, that as we know that Jesus communicates His whole life in us, He also out of that prayerfulness which is His alone breathes into us our praying.

To many a believer a new epoch in his spiritual life took place when it was revealed to him how truly and entirely Christ was his life, standing good as surety for his remaining faithful and obedient. It was then first that he really began to live a *faith-life*. No less blessed will be the discovery that Christ is surety for our prayer life too, the center and embodiment of all prayer, to be communicated by Him through the Holy Spirit to His people. "He ever liveth to make intercession" as the Head of the body, as the Leader in that new and living way that He has opened up, as the Author and the Perfecter of our faith. He provides in everything for the life of His redeemed ones by giving His own life in them: He cares for their life of prayer, by taking them up into His heavenly prayer life, by giving and maintaining His prayer life within them. "I have prayed for thee," not to render Your faith needless, but "that *thy faith* fail not": our faith and prayer of faith is rooted in His. It is "if ye abide in me," the everliving Intercessor, and pray with me and in me: "ask whatsoever ye will, and it shall be done unto you."

The thought of our fellowship in the intercession of Jesus reminds us of what He has taught us more than once before, how all these wonderful prayer promises have as their aim and their justification, the glory of God in the manifestation of His kingdom and the salvation of sinners. As long as we only or chiefly pray for ourselves, the promises of the last night must remain a sealed book to us. It is to the fruit-bearing branches of the Vine; it is to disciples sent into the world as the Father sent Him, to live for perishing men; it is to His faithful servants and intimate friends who take up the work He leaves behind, who have like their Lord become as the seedcorn, losing its life to multiply it many times—it is to such that the promises are given. Let us each find out what the work is, and which souls are entrusted to our special prayers; let us make our intercession for them our life of fellowship with God, and we shall not only find the promises of power in prayer made true to us, but we shall then first begin to realize how our abiding in Christ and His abiding in us makes us share in His own joy of blessing and saving men.

O most wonderful intercession of our blessed Lord Jesus, to which we not only owe everything, but in which we are taken up as active partners and fellow workers! Now we understand what it is to pray in the name of Jesus, and why it has such power. In His name, in His spirit, in Himself, in perfect union with Him. O wondrous, ever active, and most efficacious intercession of the man Christ Jesus! When shall we be wholly taken up into it, and always pray in it?

*   *   *   *   *

Blessed Lord, in lowly adoration I would again bow before You. Your whole redemption work has now passed into prayer: all that now occupies You in maintaining and dispensing what You purchased with Your blood is only prayer. You ever live to pray. And because we are and abide in You, the direct access to the Father is always open, our life can be one of unceasing prayer, and the answer to our prayer is sure.

Blessed Lord, You have invited Your people to be Your fellow-workers in a life of prayer. You have united Yourself with Your people and make them as Your body share with You in that ministry of intercession through which alone the world can be filled with the fruit of Your redemption and the glory of the Father. With more liberty than ever I come to You, my Lord, and beseech You: Teach me to pray. Your life is prayer, Your life is mine. Lord, teach me to pray, in You, like You.

And, O my Lord! give me especially to know, as You promised Your disciples, that You are in the Father, and I in You, and You in me. Let the uniting power of the Holy Spirit make my whole life an abiding in You and Your intercession, so that my prayer may be its echo, and the Father hear me in You and You in me. Lord Jesus! let Your mind in everything be in me, and my life in everything be in You. So shall I be prepared to be the channel through which Your intercession pours its blessing on the world. Amen.

27 *Christk the High Priest*

Father, I desire that they also whom thou hast given me be with me where I am.

John 17:24

In His parting address, Jesus gives His disciples the full revelation of what the new life was to be, when once the kingdom of God had come in power. In the indwelling of the Holy Spirit, in union with Him the heavenly Vine, in their going forth to witness and to suffer for Him, they were to find their calling and their blessedness. In between His setting forth of their future new life, the Lord had repeatedly given the most unlimited promises as to the power their prayers might have. And now in closing, He Himself proceeds to pray. To let His disciples have the joy of knowing what His intercession for them in heaven as their High Priest will be, He gives this precious legacy of His prayer to the Father. He does this at the same time because they as priests are to share in His work of intercession, that they and we might know how to perform this holy work. From the teaching of our Lord on this last night, we have learned to understand that these astonishing prayer promises have not been given in our own behalf, but in the interest of the Lord and His kingdom: it is from the Lord Himself alone that we can learn what the prayer in His name is to be. We have understood that to pray in His name is to pray in perfect unity with Himself: the high priestly prayer will teach all that the prayer in the name of Jesus may ask and expect.

This prayer is ordinarily divided into three parts. Our Lord first prays for Himself (vv. 1-5), then for His disciples (vv. 6-19), and last for all the believing people through all ages (vv. 20-26). The follower of Jesus, who gives himself to the work of intercession, and would try how much of blessing he can pray down on his circle in the name of Jesus, will in all humility let himself be led of the Spirit to study this wonderful prayer as one of the most important lessons of the school of prayer.

First of all, Jesus prays for Himself, for His being glorified, that so He may glorify the Father. "Father! glorify Thy Son. And now, Father, glorify Me." And He brings forward the grounds on which He prays. A holy covenant had been concluded between the Father and the Son in heaven. The Father had promised Him power over all flesh as the reward of His work: He had done the work, He had glorified the Father, and His one purpose is now still further to glorify Him. With utmost boldness He asks that the Father may glorify Him, that He may now be and do for His people all He has undertaken.

Disciple of Jesus, here you have the first lesson in your work of priestly intercession, to be learned from the example of your great High Priest. To pray in the name of Jesus is to pray in unity, in sympathy with Him. As the Son began His prayer by making clear His relation to the Father, pleading His work and obedience and His desire to see the Father glorified, so should you. Draw near and appear before the Father in Christ. Plead His finished work. Say that you are one with it, that you trust in it, live in it. Say that you too have given yourself to finish the work the Father has given you to do, and to live alone for His glory. And ask then confidently that the Son may be glorified in you. This is praying in the name, in the very words, in the Spirit of Jesus, in union with Jesus Himself. Such prayer has power. If with Jesus you glorify the Father, the Father will glorify Jesus by doing what you ask in His name. It is only when your own personal relation on this point, like Christ's, is clear with God, when you are glorifying Him, and seeking all for His glory, that, like Christ, you will have power to intercede for those around you.

Our Lord next prays for the circle of His disciples. He speaks of them as those whom the Father has given Him. Their chief mark is that they have received Christ's word. He says of them that He now sends them into the world in His place, just as the Father had sent Himself. And He asks two things for them: that the Father keep them from the evil one, and sanctify them through His Word, because He sanctifies Himself for them.

Just like the Lord, each believing intercessor has his own immediate circle for whom he first prays. Parents have their children, teachers their pupils, pastors their flocks, all workers their special charge, all believers those whose care lies upon their hearts. It is of great consequence that intercession should be personal, pointed, and definite. And then, our first prayer must always be that they may receive the word. But this prayer will not avail unless with our Lord we say, "I have given them Thy word": it is this that gives us liberty and power in intercession for souls. We must not only pray for them, but speak to them. And when they have received the word, let us pray much for their being kept from the evil one, for their being sanctified through that word. Instead of being hopeless or judging or giving up those who fall, let us pray for our circle, "Father! keep them in Thy name"; "Sanctify them through Thy truth." Prayer in the name of Jesus avails much: "What ye will shall be done unto you."

And then follows our Lord's prayer for a still wider circle. "I pray not only for these, but for them who through their word shall believe." His priestly heart enlarges itself to embrace all places and all time, and He prays that all who belong to Him may everywhere be one, as God's proof to the world of the divinity of His mission, and then that they may ever be with Him in His glory. Until then "that the love wherewith thou lovedst me may be in them, and I in them."

The disciple of Jesus, who has first in his own circle proved the power of prayer, cannot confine himself within its limits: he prays for the church universal and its different branches. He prays especially for the unity of the Spirit and of love. He prays for its being one in Christ, as a witness to the world that Christ, who has wrought such a wonder as to make love triumph over selfishness and separation, is indeed the Son of God sent from heaven. Every believer ought to pray much that the unity of the church, not in external organizations, but in spirit and in truth, may be made manifest.

So much for the matter of the prayer. Now for its mode. Jesus says, "Father! I Will." On the ground of His right as Son, and the Father's promise to Him, and His finished work, He might do so. The Father had said to Him, "Ask of me, and I will give thee." He simply availed Himself of the Father's promise. Jesus has given us a like promise: "*Whatsoever ye will* shall be done unto you." He asks me in His name to say what I will. Abiding in Him, in a living union with Him in which man is nothing and Christ all, the believer has the liberty to take up that word of His High Priest and, in answer to the question, "What wilt thou?" to say, "Father, I Will all that Thou hast promised." This is nothing but true faith; this is honoring God: to be assured that such confidence in saying what I will is indeed acceptable to Him. At first sight, our heart shrinks from the expression; we feel neither the liberty nor the power to speak in this way. It is a word for which alone in the most entire abnegation of our will grace will be given, but for which grace will most assuredly be given to each one who loses his will in his Lord's. He who loses his will shall find it; he who gives up his will entirely shall find it again renewed and strengthened with a divine strength. "Father, I Will:" this is the keynote of the everlasting, ever-active, all-prevailing intercession of our Lord in heaven. It is only in union with Him that our prayer avails; in union with Him it avails much. If we but abide in Him, living and walking, and doing all things in His name; if we but come and bring each separate petition, tested and touched by His Word and Spirit, and cast it into the mighty stream of intercession that goes up from Him, to be borne upward and presented before the Father, we shall have the full confidence that we receive the petitions we ask: the "Father, *I Will*" will be breathed into us by the Spirit Himself. We shall lose ourselves in Him, and become nothing, to find that in our impotence we have power and will prevail.

Disciples of Jesus, called to be like your Lord in His priestly intercession, when, O when, shall we awaken to the glory, passing all conception, of this our destiny to plead and prevail with God for perishing men? When shall we shake off the sloth that clothes itself with the pretense of humility, and yield ourselves wholly to God's Spirit, that He may fill our wills with light and with power, to know, and to take, and to possess all that our God is waiting to give to a will that lays hold on Him.

* * * * *

O my blessed High Priest, who am I that You should invite me to share with You in Your power of prevailing intercession! And why, O my Lord, am I so slow of heart to understand and believe and exercise this wonderful privilege to which You have redeemed Your people. O Lord, give Your grace that this may increasingly be my unceasing life work—in praying without ceasing to draw down the blessing of heaven on all my surroundings on earth.

Blessed Lord! I come now to accept this my calling. For this I would forsake all and follow You. Into Your hands I would believingly yield my whole being: form, train, inspire me to be one of Your prayer legion, wrestlers who watch and strive in prayer, Israels, God's princes, who have power and prevail. Take possession of my heart, and fill it with the one desire for the glory of God in the ingathering, and sanctification, and union of those whom the Father has given You. Take my mind and let this be my study and my wisdom, to know when prayer can bring a blessing. Take me wholly and fit me as a priest ever to stand before God and to bless in His name.

Blessed Lord, be it here, as through all the spiritual life: You all, I nothing. And be it here my experience too that he who has and seeks nothing for himself, receives all, even to the wonderful grace of sharing with You in Your everlasting ministry of intercession. Amen.

28 *Christic the Sacrifice*

And he said, Abba, Father, all things are possible unto Thee; remove this cup from me: howbeit not what I will, but what thou wilt.

Mark 14:36

What a contrast within the space of a few hours! What a transition from the quiet elevation of that "He lifted up his eyes to heaven, and said, Father, I Will," to that falling on the ground and crying in agony, "My Father! not what I will." In the one we see the High Priest within the veil in His all-prevailing intercession; in the other, the sacrifice on the altar opening the way through the rent veil. The high-priestly "Father, I will," in order of time precedes the sacrificial "Father, not what I will"; but this was only by anticipation, to show what the intercession would be when once the sacrifice was brought. In reality it was that prayer at the altar, "Father, not what I will," in which the prayer before the throne, "Father, I will," had its origin and its power. It is from the entire surrender of His will in Gethsemane that the High Priest on the throne has the power to ask what He will, has the right to make His people share in that power too, and ask what they will.

For all who would learn to pray in the school of Jesus, this Gethsemane lesson is one of the most sacred and precious. To a superficial scholar it may appear to take away the courage to pray in faith. If even the earnest supplication of the Son was not heard, if even the Beloved had to say, "Not what I will!" how much more do we need to speak so. And thus it appears impossible that the promises that the Lord had given only a few hours previously, "Whatsoever ye shall ask," "Whatsoever ye will," could have been meant literally. A deeper insight into the meaning of Gethsemane would teach us that we have here the sure ground and the open way to the assurance of an answer to our prayer. Let us draw nigh in reverent and adoring wonder, to gaze on this great sight— God's Son thus offering up prayer and supplications with strong crying and tears, and not obtaining what He asks. He is our Teacher, and will open up to us the mystery of His holy sacrifice, as revealed in this wondrous prayer.

To understand the prayer, let us note the infinite difference between what our Lord prayed earlier as a royal Priest, and what He here supplicates in His weakness. Before, it was for the glorifying of the Father He prayed, and the glorifying of Himself and His people as the fulfillment of distinct promises that had been given Him. He asks what He knew to be according to the word and the will of the Father; He might boldly say, "Father, I will." Now He prays for something in regard to which the Father's will is not yet clear to Him. As far as He knows, it is the Father's will that He should drink the cup. He had told His disciples of the cup He must drink: a little later He would again say, "The cup which my Father hath given me, shall I not drink it?" It was for this He had come to this earth. But when, in the unutterable agony of soul that burst upon Him as the power of darkness came upon Him, and He began to taste the first drops of death as the wrath of God against sin, His human nature, as it shuddered in presence of the awful reality of being made a curse, gave utterance in this cry of anguish, to its desire that, if God's purpose could be accomplished without it, He might be spared the awful cup: "Let this cup pass from me." That desire was the evidence of the intense reality of His humanity. The "not as I will" kept that desire from being sinful: as He pleadingly cries, "All things are possible with thee," and returns again to still more earnest prayer that the cup may be removed, it is His thrice-repeated "Not what I will" that constitutes the very essence and worth of His sacrifice. He had asked for something of which He could not say: I know it is Thy will. He had pleaded God's power and love, and had then withdrawn it in His final "thy will be done." The prayer that the cup should pass away could not be answered; the prayer of submission that God's will be done was heard, and gloriously answered in His victory first over the fear, and then over the power of death.

It is in this denial of His will, this complete surrender of His will to the will of the Father, that Christ's obedience reached its highest perfection. It is from the sacrifice of the will in Gethsemane that the sacrifice of the life on Calvary derives its value. It is here, as Scripture says, that He learned obedience, and became the author of everlasting salvation to all who obey Him. It was because He there, in that prayer, became obedient to death, even the death of the cross, that God has highly exalted Him, and given Him the power to ask what He will. It was in that "Father, not what I will," that He obtained the power for the other "Father, I will." It was by Christ's submission in Gethsemane that His will not be done, that He secured for His people the right to say to them, "Ask whatsoever ye will."

Let me look at them again, the deep mysteries that Gethsemane offers to my view. There is the first: the Father offers His well-beloved the cup, the cup of wrath. The second: the Son, always so obedient, shrinks back, and implores that He may not have to drink it. The third: the Father does not grant the Son His request, but still gives the cup. And then the last: the Son yields His will, is content that His will be not done, and goes out to Calvary to drink the cup. O Gethsemane, in you I see how my Lord could give me such unlimited assurance of an answer to my prayers. As my surety He won it for me, by His consent to have His petition unanswered.

This is in harmony with the whole scheme of redemption. Our Lord always wins for us the opposite of what He suffered. He was bound that we might go free. He was made sin that we might become the righteousness of God. He died that we might live. He bore God's curse that God's blessing might be ours. He endured the not answering of His prayer, that our prayers might find an answer. Yes, He spake, "Not as I will," that He might say to us, "If ye abide in me, ask what ye will; it shall be done unto you."

144

Yes, "If ye abide in me"; here in Gethsemane the word acquires new force and depth. Christ is our Head, who as surety stands in our place, and bears what we must forever have borne. We had deserved that God should turn a deaf ear to us, and never listen to our cry. Christ comes, and suffers this too for us: He suffers what we had merited; for our sins He suffers beneath the burden of that unanswered prayer. But now His suffering avails this for me: what He has borne is taken away from me; His merit has won for me the answer to every prayer, if I abide in Him.

Yes, in Him, as He bows there in Gethsemane, I must abide. As my Head, He not only once suffered for me, but ever lives in me, breathing and working His own disposition in me too. The Eternal Spirit, through which He offered Himself to God, is the Spirit that dwells in me too, and makes me partaker of the very same obedience, and the sacrifice of the will to God. That Spirit teaches me to yeild my will entirely to the will of the Father, to give it up even unto the death, in Christ to be dead to it. Whatever is my own mind and thought and will, even though it is not directly sinful, He teaches me to fear and flee. He opens my ear to wait in great gentleness and teachableness of soul for what the Father has day by day to speak and to reach. He reveals to me how union with God's will in the love of it, is union with God Himself; how entire surrender to God's will is the Father's claim, the Son's example and the true blessedness of the soul. He leads my will into the fellowship of Christ's death and resurrection, my will dies in Him, in Him to be made alive again. He breathes into it, as a renewed and quickened will, a holy insight into God's perfect will, a holy joy in yielding itself to be an instrument of that will, a holy liberty and power to lay hold of God's will to answer prayer. With my whole will I learn to live for the interests of God and His kingdom, to exercise the power of that will—crucified but risen again in nature and in prayer, on earth and in heaven, with men and with God. The more deeply I enter into the "Father, not what I will" of Gethsemane, and into Him who spake it, to abide in Him, the fuller is my spiritual access into the power of His "Father, I will." And the soul experiences that it is the will, which has become nothing that God's will may be all, which now becomes inspired with a divine strength to really will what God wills, and to claim what has been promised it in the name of Christ.

Let us listen to Christ in Gethsemane, as He calls, "If ye abide in me, ask whatsoever ye will, and it shall be done unto you." Being of one mind and spirit with Him in His giving up everything to God's will, living like Him in obedience and surrender to the Father; this is abiding in Him; this is the secret of power in prayer.

*　*　*　*　*

Blessed Lord Jesus, Gethsemane was Your school, where You learned to pray and to obey. It is still Your school, where You lead all Your disciples who desire to learn to obey and to pray even as You. Lord, teach me there to pray, in the faith that You have atoned for and conquered our self-will, and can indeed give us grace to pray like You.

O Lamb of God, I would follow You to Gethsemane, there to become one with You, and to abide in You as You do to the very death yield Your will to the Father. With You, through You, in You, I yield my will in absolute and entire surrender to the will of the Father. Conscious of my own weakness, and the secret power with which self-will would assert itself and again take its place on the throne, I claim in faith the power of Your victory. You triumphed over it and deliver me from it. In Your death I would daily live: in Your life I would daily die. Abiding in You, let my will, through the power of Your eternal Spirit, only be the tuned instrument that yields to every touch of the will of my God. With my whole soul do I say with You and in You, "Father, not as I will, but as Thou wilt."

And then, blessed Lord, open my heart and that of all Your people to take in fully the glory of the truth, that a will given up to God is a will accepted of God to be used in His service, to desire, and purpose, and determine, and will what is according to God's will. A will which, in the power of the Holy Spirit the indwelling God, is to exercise its royal prerogative in prayer, to loose and to bind in heaven and on earth, to ask whatever it will, and to say it shall be done.

O Lord Jesus, teach me to pray. Amen.

29 Our Boldness in Prayer

And this is the boldness which we have toward him, that if we ask anything according to His will, He beareth us: And if we know that he heareth us whatsoever we ask, we know that we have the petitions which we have asked of him.

1 John 5:14, 15

One of the greatest hindrances to believing prayer with many is undoubtedly this: they do not know if what they ask is according to the will of God. As long as they are in doubt on this point, they cannot have the boldness to ask in the assurance that they certainly shall receive. And they soon begin to think that, if once they have made known their requests and receive no answer, it is best to leave it to God to do according to His good pleasure. The words of John, "If we ask anything *according to his will,* he heareth us," as they understand them, make certainty as to answer to prayer impossible, because they cannot be sure of what really may be the will of God. They think of God's will as His hidden counsel—how should man be able to fathom what really may be the purpose of the all-wise God.

This is the opposite of what John aimed at in writing this way. He wished to rouse us to boldness, to confidence, to full assurance of faith in prayer. He says, "*This is the boldness which we have toward Him,*" that we can say: Father, You know and I know that I ask according to Your will: I know You hear me. "This is the boldness, that if we ask anything according to his will, he heareth us." On this account He adds at once: "If we know that he heareth us whatsoever we ask, we *know,*" through this faith, "that we have," that now, while we pray, we receive "the petition," the special things, "we have asked of him." John supposes that when we pray, we first find out if our prayers are according to the will of God. They may be according to God's will, and yet not come at once, or without the persevering prayer of faith. It is to give us courage to persevere and to be strong in faith, that He tells us. This gives us boldness or confidence in prayer, if we ask anything according to His will, He hears us. It is evident that if it be a matter of uncertainty to us whether our petitions are according to His will, we cannot have the comfort of what he says, "We know that we have the petitions which we have asked of him."

But this is the difficulty. More than one believer says: "I do not know if what I desire is according to the will of God. God's will is the purpose of His infinite wisdom: it is impossible for me to know whether He may not count something else better for me than what I desire, or may not have some reasons for withholding what I ask." Everyone feels how with such thoughts the prayer of faith, of which Jesus said, "Whatsoever shall believe that *these things which he saith* shall come to pass, he shall have *whatsoever* he saith," becomes an impossibility. There may be the prayer of submission, and of trust in God's wisdom; there cannot be the prayer of faith. The great mistake here is that God's children do not really believe that it is possible to know His will. Or if they believe this, they do not take the time and trouble to find it out. What we need is to see clearly in what way it is that the Father leads His waiting, teachable child to know that his petition is according to His will. It is through God's holy word, taken up and kept in the heart, the life, the will; and through God's Holy Spirit, accepted in His indwelling and leading, that we shall learn to know that our petitions are according to His will.

Through the word. There is a secret will of God, with which we often fear that our prayers may be at variance. It is not with this will of God, but His will as revealed in His word, that we have to do in prayer. Our notions of what the secret will may have decreed, and of how it might render the answers to our prayers impossible, are mostly very erroneous. Child-like faith as to what He is willing to do for His children, simply keeps to the Father's assurance, that it is His will to hear prayer and to do what faith in His word desires and accepts. In the word the Father has revealed in general promises the great principles of His will with His people. The child has to take the promise and apply it to the special circumstances in His life to which it has reference. Whatever he asks within the limits of that revealed will, he can know to be according to the will of God, and he may confidently expect. In His word, God has given us the revelation of His will and plans with us, with His people, and with the world, with the most precious promises of the grace and power with which through His people He will carry out His plans and do His work. As faith becomes strong and bold enough to claim the fulfillment of the general promise in the special case, we may have the assurance that our prayers are heard: they are according to God's will. Take the words of John in the verse following our text as an illustration: "If any man see his brother sinning a sin not unto death, he shall ask, and *God will give him life.*" Such is the general promise; and the believer who pleads on the ground of this promise, prays according to the will of God, and John would give him boldness to know that he has the petition that he asks.

But this apprehension of God's will is something spiritual, and must be spiritually discerned. It is not as a matter of logic that we can argue it out: God has said it; I must have it. Nor has every Christian the same gift or calling. While the general will revealed in the promise is the same for all, there is for each one a special different will according to God's purpose. And herein is the wisdom of the saints, to know this special will of God for each of us, according to the measure of grace given us, and so to ask in prayer just what God has prepared and made possible for each. It is to communicate this wisdom *that the Holy Spirit dwells in us.* The personal application of the general promises of the word to our special personal needs—*it is for this that the leading of the Holy Spirit is given us.*

It is this union of the teaching of the word and Spirit that many do not understand, and so there is a twofold difficulty in knowing what God's will may be. Some seek the will of God in an inner feeling or conviction, and would have the Spirit lead them without the word. Others seek it in the word, without the living leading of the Holy Spirit. The two must be united: only in the word, only in the Spirit, but in these most surely, can we know the will of God, and learn to pray according to it. In the heart the word and Spirit must meet: it is only by indwelling that we can experience their teaching. The word must dwell, must abide in us: heart and life must day by day be under its influence. Not from without, but from within, comes the quickening of the word by the Spirit. It is only he who yields himself entirely in his whole life to the supremacy of the word and the will of God, who can expect in special cases to discern what that word and will permit him boldly to ask. And even as with the word, so with the Spirit: if I would have the leading of the Spirit in prayer to assure me what God's will is, my whole life must be yielded to that leading; so only can mind and heart become spiritual and capable of knowing God's holy will. It is he who, through word and Spirit, *lives in the will* of God by doing it, who will know to pray according to that will in the confidence that He hears us.

Would that Christians might see what incalculable harm they do themselves by the thought that because possibly their prayer is not according to God's will, they must be content without an answer. God's word tells us that the great reason of unanswered prayer is that we do not pray aright: "Ye ask and receive not, because ye ask amiss." In not granting an answer, the Father tells us that there is something wrong in our praying. He wants to teach us to find it out and confess it, and so to educate us to true believing and prevailing prayer. He can attain His object only when He brings us to see that we are to blame for the withholding of the answer; our aim, or our faith, or our life is not what it should be. But this purpose of God is frustrated as long as we are content to say: It is perhaps because my prayer is not according to His will that He does not hear me. O let us no longer throw the blame of our unanswered prayers on the secret will of God, but on our own praying amiss. Let that word, "Ye receive not, because ye ask amiss," be as the lantern of the Lord, searching heart and life to prove that we are indeed such as those to whom Christ gave His promises of certain answers. Let us believe that we *can know* if our prayer is according to God's will. Let us yield our heart to have the word of the Father dwell richly there, to have Christ's word abiding in us. Let us live day by day with the anointing that teaches all things. Let us yield ourselves unreservedly to the Holy Spirit as He teaches us to abide in Christ, to dwell in the Father's presence, and we shall soon understand how the Father's love longs that the child should know His will, and should, in the confidence that that will includes all that His power and love have promised to do, know too that He hears the petitions that we ask of Him. "*This is* the boldness which we have, that if we ask anything according to his will, he heareth us."

* * * * *

Blessed Master, with my whole heart I thank You for this blessed lesson, that the path to a life full of answers to prayer is through the will of God. Lord, teach me to know this blessed will by living it, loving it, and always doing it. So shall I learn to offer prayers according to that will, and to find in their harmony with God's blessed will, my boldness in prayer and my confidence in accepting the answer.

Father! *it is Your will* that Your child should enjoy Your presence and blessing. *It is Your will* that everything in the life of Your child should be in accordance with Your will, and that the Holy Spirit should work this in Him. *It is Your will* that Your child should live in the daily experience of distinct answers to prayer, so as to enjoy living and direct fellowship with Yourself. *It is Your will* that Your name should be glorified in and through Your children, and that it will be in those who trust You. O my Father, let this Your will be my confidence is all I ask.

Blessed Savior, teach me to believe in the glory of this will. That will is the eternal love, which with divine power works out its purpose in each human will that yields itself to it. Lord, teach me this. You can make me see how every promise and every command of the word is indeed the will of God, and that its fulfillment is secured to me by God Himself. Let thus the will of God become to me the sure rock on which my prayer and my assurance of an answer ever rests. Amen.

30 The Ministry of Intercession

A holy priesthood, to offer up spiritual sacrifices, acceptable to God through Jesus Christ.

1 Peter 2:5

Ye shall be named the priests of the Lord.

Isaiah 61:6

The Spirit of the LORD God is upon me, because the LORD hath anointed me." These are the words of Jesus in Isaiah. As the fruit of His work all redeemed ones are priests, fellow partakers with Him of His anointing with the Spirit as High Priest. "Like the precious ointment upon the beard of Aaron, that went down to the skirts of his garments." As every son of Aaron, so every member of Jesus' body has a right to the priesthood. But not every one exercises it: many are still entirely ignorant of it. And yet it is the highest privilege of a child of God, the mark of greatest nearness and likess to Him, "who ever liveth to pray," Do you doubt if this really is so? Think of what constitutes priesthood.

There is, first, the *work* of the priesthood. This has two sides, one godward, the other manward. "Every priest . . . is *ordained for men* in things *pertaining to God*" (Heb. 5:1); or, as it is said by Moses (Deut. 10:8, see also 21:5, 33:10; Mal. 2:6): "The Lord separated the tribe of Levi . . . *to stand before the Lord* to minister unto him, and *to bless his name.*" On the one hand, the priest had the power to draw near to God, to dwell with Him in His house, and to present before Him the blood of the sacrifice or the burning incense. This work he did not do, however, on his own behalf, but for the sake of the people whose representative he was. This is the other side of his work. He received from the people their sacrifices, presented them before God, and then came out to bless His name, to give the assurance of His favor and to teach them His law.

A priest is therefore a man who does not at all live for himself. *He lives with God and for God.* His work is as God's servant to care for His house, His honor, and His worship, to make known to men His love and His will. *He lives with men and for men* (Heb. 5:2). His work is to find out their sin and need, and to bring it before God, to offer sacrifice and incense in their name, to obtain forgiveness and blessing for them, and then to come out and bless them in His name. This is the high calling of every believer. "Such honour have all his saints." They have been redeemed with the one purpose to be in the midst of the perishing millions around them God's priests, who in conformity to Jesus, the great High Priest, are to be the ministers and stewards of the grace of God to all around them.

And then there is the *walk* of the priesthood, in harmony with its work. As God is holy, so the priest was to be especially holy. This means not only separated from everything unclean, but *holy to God,* being set apart and given up to God for His disposal. The separation from the world and setting apart to God was indicated in many ways.

It was seen in the clothing: the holy garments, made after God's own order, marked them as His (Exod. 28). It was seen in the command as to their special purity and freedom from all contact from death and defilement (Lev. 21:22). Much that was allowed to an ordinary Israelite was forbidden to them. It was seen in the injunction that the priest must have no bodily defect or blemish; bodily perfection was to be the type of wholeness and holiness in God's service. And it was seen in the arrangement by which the priestly tribes were to have no inheritance with the other tribes; God was to be their inheritance. Their life was to be one of faith: set apart to God, they were to live on Him as well as for Him.

All this is the emblem of what the character of the New Testament priest is to be. Our priestly power with God depends on our personal life and walk. We must be of them of whose walk on earth Jesus says, "They have not defiled their garments."

In the surrender of what my appear lawful to others in our separation from the world, we must prove that our consecration to be holy to the Lord is wholehearted and entire. The bodily perfection of the priest must have its counterpart in our too being "without spot or blemish"; "the man of God perfect, throughly furnished unto all good works," "perfect and entire, wanting nothing" (Lev. 21:17-21; Eph. 5:27; 2 Tim. 2:7; Jas. 1:4). And above all, we consent to give up all inheritance on earth; to forsake all, and like Christ to have only God as our portion, to possess as not possessing, and hold all for God alone; it is this that marks the true priest, the man who only lives for God and his fellow men.

And now the *way* to the priesthood. In Aaron God had chosen all his sons to be priests: each of them was a priest by birth. And yet he could not enter on his work without a special act of ordinance—his consecration. Every child of God is priest in right of his birth, his blood relationship to the great High Priest; but this is not enough: he will exercise his power only as he accepts and realizes his consecration.

With Aaron and his sons it took place in this way (Exod. 29): After being washed and clothed, they were anointed with the holy oil. Sacrifices were then offered, and the right ear, the right hand, and the right foot were touched with the blood. Then they and their garments were once again sprinkled with the blood and the oil together. And so it is as the child of God enters more fully into what the blood and the spirit of which he already is partaker, are to him, that the power of the holy priesthood will work in him. The blood will take away all sense of unworthiness; the Spirit, all sense of unfitness.

Let us notice what there was new in the application of the blood to the priest. If ever he had as a penitent brought a sacrifice for his sin, seeking forgiveness, the blood was sprinkled on the altar, but not on his person. But now, for priestly consecration, there was to be closer contact with the blood; ear and hand and foot were by a special act brought under its power, and the whole being taken possession of and sanctified for God. And so, when the believer, who had been content to think chiefly of the blood sprinkled on the mercy seat as what he needed for pardon, is led to seek full priestly access to God, he feels the need for a fuller and more abiding experience of the power of the blood, as really sprinkling and cleansing the heart from an evil conscience, so that he has "no more conscience of sin" (Heb 10:2), as cleansing from all sin. And it is as he gets to enjoy this, that the consciousness is awakened of his wonderful right of most intimate access to God, and of the full assurance that his intercessions are acceptable.

And as the blood gives the right, the Spirit gives the power, and fits for believing intercession. He breathes into us the priestly spirit—burning love for God's honor and the saving of souls. He makes us so one with Jesus that prayer in His name is a reality. He strengthens us to believing, importunate prayer. The more the Christian is truly filled with the Spirit of Christ, the more spontaneous will be his giving himself up to the life of priestly intercession. Beloved fellow-Christians, God needs, greatly needs, priests who can draw near to Him, who live in His presence, and by their intercession draw down the blessings of His grace on others. And the world needs, greatly needs, priests who will bear the burden of the perishing ones, and intercede on their behalf.

Are you willing to offer yourself for this holy work? You know the surrender it demands—nothing less than the Christlike giving up of all, that the saving purposes of God's love may be accomplished among men. Oh, be no longer of those who are content if they have salvation, and just do work enough to keep themselves warm and lively. Let nothing keep you back from giving yourselves to be wholly and only priests— nothing else, nothing less than the priests of the Most High God. the thought of unworthiness, of unfitness, need not keep you back. In *the blood*, the objective power of the perfect redemption works in you: in *the Spirit*, its full subjective personal experience as a divine life is secured. *The blood* provides an infinite worthiness to make your prayers most acceptable: *the Spirit* provides a divine fitness, teaching you to pray just according to the will of God. *Every priest knew that when he presented a sacrifice according to the law of the sanctuary, it was accepted;* under the covering of the blood and Spirit you have the assurance that all the wonderful promises to prayer in the name of Jesus will be fulfilled in you. Abiding in union with the great High Priest, "you shall ask what you will, and it shall be done unto you." You will have power to pray the effectual prayer of the righteous man that avails much. You will not only join in the general prayer of the church for the world, but be able in your own sphere to take up your special work in prayer—as priests,to transact it with God, to receive and know the answer, and so to bless in His name. Come, brother, come, and be a priest, *only* priest, *all* priest. Seek now to walk before the Lord in the full consciousness that you have been set apart for the holy ministry in intercession. This is the true blessedness of conformity to the image of God's Son.

* * * * *

O blessed High Priest, accept the consecration in which my soul now would respond to Your message.

I believe in the holy priesthood of Your saints, and that I too am a priest, with power to appear before the Father, and in the prayer that avails much bring down blessing on the perishing around me.

I believe in the power of Your precious blood to cleanse from all sin, to give me perfect confidence toward God, and bring me near in the full assurance of faith that my intercession will be heard.

I believe in the anointing of the Spirit, coming down daily from You, my great High Priest, to sanctify me, to fill me with the consciousness of my priestly calling, and with love to souls, to teach me what is according to God's will, and how to pray the prayer of faith.

I believe that, as You my Lord Jesus are Yourself in all things my life, so You, too are the surety for my prayer-life, and will Yourself draw me up into the fellowship of Your wondrous work of intercession.

In this faith I yield myself this day to my God, as one of His anointed priests, to stand before His face to intercede in behalf of sinners, and to come out and bless in His name.

Holy Lord Jesus, accept and seal my consecration. Yes, Lord, lay Your hands on me, and consecrate me to this Your holy work. And let me walk among men with the consciousness and the character of a priest of the most high God.

Unto Him who loved us, and washed us from our sins in His own blood, and has made us kings and priests to God and His Father; to Him be glory and dominion for ever and ever. Amen.

31 *A Life of Prayer*

Rejoice always; pray without ceasing; in everything give thanks.

1 Thessalonians 5:16, 17, 18

Our Lord spoke the parable of the widow and the unjust judge to teach us that men ought to pray always and not give up. As the widow persevered in seeking one definite thing, the parable appears to have reference to persevering prayer for some one blessing, when God delays or appears to refuse. The words in the Epistles, which speak of continuing in prayer and watching in the same, of praying always in the Spirit, appear more to refer to the whole life being one of prayer. As the soul is filling with the longing for the manifestation of God's glory to us and in us, through us and around us, and with the confidence that He hears the prayers of His children, the inmost life of the soul is continually rising upward in dependence and faith, in longing desire and trustful expectation.

At the close of this book it will not be difficult to say what is needed to live such a life of prayer. The first thing is undoubtedly the entire sacrifice of the life to God's kingdom and glory. He who seeks to pray without ceasing because he wants to be very pious and good, will never attain it. It is the forgetting of self and yielding ourselves to live for God and His honor that enlarges the heart, that teaches us to regard everything in the light of God and His will, and that instinctively recognizes in everything around us the need of God's help and blessing, an opportunity for His being glorified. Because everything is weighed and tested by the one thing that fills the heart—the glory of God, and because the soul has learned that only what is of God can really be to Him and His glory, the whole life becomes a looking up, a crying from the inmost heart, for God to prove His power and love, and so show forth His glory. The believer awakes to the consciousness that he is one of the watchmen on Zion's walls, one of the Lord's remembrances, whose call really touches the moves the King in heaven to do what would otherwise not be done. He understands how real Paul's exhortation was, "praying always with all prayer and supplication in the Spirit for all the saints and for me," and "continue in prayer, withal praying also for us." To forget oneself, to live for God and His kingdom among men, is the way to learn to pray without ceasing.

This life devoted to God must be accompanied by the deep confidence that our prayer is effectual. We have seen how our blessed Lord insisted on nothing so much in His prayer lessons as faith in the Father as a God who most certainly does what we ask. "Ask and ye shall receive"; count confidently on an answer, is with Him the beginning and the end of His teaching (compare Matt. 7:8 and John 16:24). In proportion as this assurance masters us, and it becomes a settled thing that our prayers tell and that God does what we ask, we dare not neglect the use of this wonderful power: the soul turns wholly to God, and our life becomes prayer. We see that the Lord needs and takes time, because we and all around us are the creatures of time, under the law of growth; but knowing that not one single prayer of faith can possibly be lost, that there is sometimes a needs-be for the storing up and accumulating prayer, that persevering prayer is irresistible, prayer becomes the quiet, persistent living of our life of desire and faith in the presence of our God. O do not let us any longer by our reasonings limit and enfeeble such free and sure promises of the living God, robbing them of their power, and ourselves of the wonderful confidence they are meant to inspire. Not in God, not in His secret will, not in the limitations of His promises, but in us, in ourselves is the hindrance; we are not what we should be to obtain the promise. Let us open our whole heart to God's words or promise in all their simplicity and truth: they will search us and humble us; they will lift us up and make us glad and strong. And to the faith that knows it gets what it asks, prayer is not a work or a burden, but a joy and a triumph; it becomes a necessity and a second nature.

This union of strong desire and firm confidence again is nothing but the life of the Holy Spirit within us. The Holy Spirit dwells in us, hides Himself in the depths of our being, and stirs the desire after the Unseen and the Divine, after God Himself. Now in groanings that cannot be uttered, then in clear and conscious assurance; now in special distinct petitions for the deeper revelation of Christ to ourselves, then in pleadings for a soul, a work, the church or the world, it is always and alone the Holy Spirit who draws out the heart to thirst for God, to long for His being made known and glorified. Where the child of God really lives and walks in the Spirit, where he is not content to remain carnal, but seeks to be spiritual, in everything a fit organ for the divine Spirit to reveal the life of Christ and Christ Himself, there the never-ceasing intercession-life of the blessed Son cannot but reveal and repeat itself in our experience. Because it is the Spirit of Christ who prays in us, our prayer must be heard; because it is we who pray in the Spirit, there is need of time, and patience, and continual renewing of the prayer, until every obstacle is conquered, and the harmony between God's Spirit and ours is perfect.

But the chief thing we need for such a life of unceasing prayer is to know that Jesus teaches us to pray. We have begun to understand a little what His teaching is. It is not the communication of new thoughts or views, not the discovery of failure or error, not the stirring up of desire and faith, of however much importance all this is, but the taking us up into the fellowship of His own prayer life before the Father—this it is by which Jesus really teaches. It was the sight of the praying Jesus that made the disciples long and ask to be taught to pray. It is the faith of the every-praying Jesus, whose alone is the power to pray, that teaches us truly to pray. We know why: He who prays is our Head and our Life. All He has is ours and is given to us when we give ourselves all to Him. By His blood He leads us into the immediate presence of God. The inner sanctuary is our home, we dwell there. And He who lives so near God, and knows that He has been brought near to bless those who are far, cannot but pray. Christ makes us partakers with Himself of His prayer power and prayer life. We understand then that our true aim must not be to work much, and have prayer enough to keep the work right, but to pray much and then to work enough for the power and blessing obtained in prayer to find its way through us to men. It is Christ who ever lives to pray, who saves and reigns. He communicates His prayer life to us: He maintains it in us if we trust Him. He is surety for our praying without ceasing. Yes, Christ teaches to pray by showing how He does it, by doing it in us, by leading us to do it in Him and like Him. Christ is all, the life and strength too for a never-ceasing prayer life. It is the sight of this, the sight of the ever-praying Christ as our life, that enables us to pray without ceasing. Because His priesthood is the power of an endless life, that resurrection life that never fades and never fails, and because His life is our life, praying without ceasing can become to us nothing less than the life joy of heaven. So the apostle says: "Rejoice *evermore;* pray *without ceasing; in everything* give thanks." Borne up between the never-ceasing joy and the never-ceasing praise, never-ceasing prayer is the manifestation of the power of the eternal life, where Jesus always prays. The union between the Vine and the branch is in very deed a prayer union. The highest conformity to Christ, the most blessed participation in the glory of His heavenly life, is that we take part in His work of intercession: He and we live ever to pray. In the experience of our union with Him, praying without ceasing becomes a possibility, a reality, the holiest and most blessed part of our holy and blessed fellowship with God. We have our abode within the veil, in the presence of the Father. What the Father says, we do: what the Son says, the Father does. Praying without ceasing is the earthly manifestation of heaven come down to us, the foretaste of the life where they rest not day or night in the song of worship and adoration.

* * * * *

O my Father, with my whole heart do I praise You for this wondrous life of never-ceasing prayer, never-ceasing fellowship, never-ceasing answers, and never-ceasing experience of my oneness with Him who ever lives to pray. O my God, keep me ever so dwelling and walking in the presence of Your glory, that prayer may be the spontaneous expression of my life with You.

Blessed Savior, with my whole heart I praise You that You came from heaven to share with me in my needs and cries, that I might share with You in Your all-prevailing intercession. And I thank You that You have taken me into the school of prayer, to teach the blessedness and the power of a life that is all prayer. And most of all, that You have taken me up into the fellowship of Your life of intercession, that through me too Your blessings may be dispensed to those around me.

Holy Spirit, with deep reverence I thank You for Your work in me. It is through You I am lifted up into a share in the intercourse between the Son and the Father, and enter so into the fellowship of the life and love of the Holy Trinity. Spirit of God, perfect Your work in me; bring me into perfect union with Christ in Intercessor. Let Your unceasing indwelling make my life one of unceasing intercession. And let my life so become one that is unceasingly to the glory of the Father and to the blessing of those around me. Amen.